Attacking Zone Defenses
In Basketball

Attacking Zone Defenses

In Basketball

JACK RICHARDS

PARKER PUBLISHING COMPANY, INC.
West Nyack, N.Y.

© 1977 by

Parker Publishing Company, Inc.

West Nyack, N.Y.

Library of Congress Cataloging in Publication Data

Richards, Jack W
    Attacking zone defenses in basketball.

    Includes index.
    1. Basketball—Offense. I. Title.
GV889.R47   796.32'32   76-57214
ISBN 0-13-050245-6

Printed in the United States of America

Dedication

To my three favorite cheerleaders:

Linda, Laurie, and Karen.

Also by the Author

Complete Handbook of Sports Scoring and Record Keeping (with Danny Hill)

HOW THIS BOOK WILL HELP YOU DEFEAT ZONE DEFENSES

For many years now I have been carefully observing the effect of zone defenses in the game of basketball. I have watched many teams totally succumb to them and others cut them apart. I began to develop a catalog of what I consider to be the effective zone offenses that I have watched or talked about with other coaches. This book represents what I have accumulated.

Within these covers is a comprehensive analysis of the zone defense in basketball. The many types of zones, with their various strengths and weaknesses, are described along with the important principles of attack against them. Following this are many methods and styles of play to use against each type of zone from which you may select the one or more that is in keeping with your philosophy and style of play.

Obviously, what's contained in this book is *my* range of experience, and is not intended to be a definitive work on zone attacks everywhere. I am confident, however, that a coach on any level and with any range of experience will find many ideas that will help him better his zone attack. Some coaches may wish to look for a particular offense that fits their style or approach to the game, or one that will meet their needs in a special situation during the season. Still others may wish to use the book as a complete guide to the development of a zone offense—it most definitely has that capacity.

For the most part, I have tried to speak in coaching language: diagrams. I trust that coaches will understand that the zone offenses presented in this book are effective in a far wider range of use than offered. The background and knowledge of each individual will enable him to see their application in a variety of ways.

I am deeply indebted to my many coaching friends who have shared with me their ideas on zone attack. Their unselfish desire to help improve the game of basketball has provided me with the inspiration necessary to produce such a work.

Jack Richards

CONTENTS

11

Attacking Zone Defenses
In Basketball

Chapter 1

ORGANIZING THE OVERALL ATTACK AGAINST SHORT ZONES

Before you begin to build an offense, it is essential that you spend a considerable amount of time analyzing all the conceivable situations your team may be forced to handle. Then you must establish certain principles of attack to govern your design.

In my opinion a team should master more than one zone attack to be totally effective. There should be at least one against the odd man fronts, one against even man fronts and an "all-purpose" attack that is the basic offense used most of the time. Also, it is necessary that certain principles of play be established to counter special defenses such as the box-and-one, diamond-and-one, and combination defenses if they should occur during the season.

In the final analysis, you need to be confident that your attack is intelligent and based solidly on sound basketball fundamentals. Success in the execution of these fundamentals is, of course, the result of many hours of hard work in practice.

The following principles should be considered:

I. SHOOTING

Every coach knows that shooting plays the major role in a zone offense. If it is not performing, all the other principles are of little help. In analyzing a loss, how many of us have complained, "We got all the shots we wanted tonight, but we just couldn't hit!"? Few things are more frustrating for a coach than to have his team miss the good percentage shots, particularly when the offensive pattern has been well executed.

An analysis of the shooting ability of each player should take place. This would include:

A. Most effective *range*.

B. Most effective shooting *area* on the court.

C. Ability to *shoot under pressure*.

D. Most effective *type* of shot.

It is imperative that the players on a team have *meaningful* shooting practices before being called upon to attack a zone defense. Considerable practice time, therefore, should be devoted to the shots from each of the areas on the court where the offense is designed to produce them. Game-type pressure must be exerted on the shooter during the shooting drill to enable him to develop his timing, a proper release, and to help him become aware of the open areas when pressure would prevent the shot.

Good percentage shooting makes sense. The whole idea behind a patterned attack is to get a good shot while balance is maintained. Passing up one shot for a better one is not an easy lesson to teach, but there are times when it is absolutely essential if success is to be maintained. The shot should never be hurried, and when the player takes it, it is with the knowledge that none of his teammates is in a better shooting position. The individual must know his own ability to score from each of the positions on the floor where he is likely to receive the shot.

II. FAST BREAK

With the exception of good outside shooting, perhaps the single most effective technique available for combating zone defenses is the fast break. The zone defense must have some time to set up to be completely effective.

Therefore, if a team can beat the zone down court and get a quick shot before the zone is organized, an obvious advantage can be gained. If the break is well-executed it should produce:

A. Deeper penetration and better percentage shots.

B. More effective offensive rebounding.

C. A reluctance by the opponent to go to his offensive boards with the same degree of strength as he would against a deliberate offense.

D. A change of tempo.

E. General disorganization or confusion in defensive assignments within the zone.

F. A means of combating the numerous changing defenses that are popular today.

G. Pressure on the opponent.

H. More balanced scoring because everyone is a potential threat.

I. A higher degree of enthusiasm and hard work on the part of most players who prefer a wide-open game.

It is beyond the scope of this book to discuss the fast break in detail. Suffice it to say that it deserves considerable attention in the coach's master plan of
. attack against the zone defense.

III. MOVEMENT OF THE BALL IN THE ATTACK

The zone defense must be forced to move. The more rapidly an offense creates new defensive problems, the more ineffective the zone will become. The easiest way to do this, of course, is to move the ball. This is not to say that the ball should be moved simply for the sake of moving it, but that each pass should create new problems for the defense to the point where the necessary adjustment is impossible.

The attacking team should avoid standardized passing lanes and the ball should be moved counter to the flow of defensive movement, if possible. The use of deceptive fakes before passing helps to create defensive flow counter to the movement of the ball. The shorter and quicker the pass, the better. There are times when a hard cross-court pass does make sense, but the coach should designate when these are and attempt to keep them to a minimum.

Success in this area requires a great deal of patience, considerable skill, intelligent thought, and anticipation. The dribble should be used quite sparingly against the zones. Driving down a lane to the basket, splitting seams to draw two defensive players to the ball, and escaping pressure are the only really practical uses for this skill.

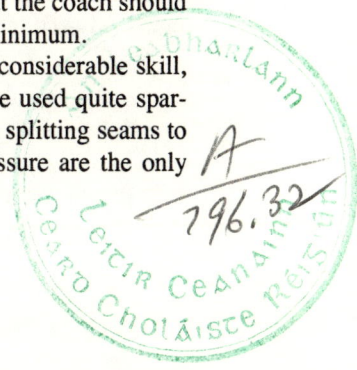

IV. MOVEMENT OF MEN IN THE ATTACK

If movement of the ball is effective, movement of the offensive men at the same time makes it doubly effective. Maintaining vision on both the ball and on the moving men creates major problems for the defense. Teams that simply stand and pass the ball, no matter how rapidly, are not utilizing all their offensive potential.

It is usually best to split defensive men when moving through a zone. Coming to the target area from behind the player is also effective because the player cannot see the movement until it is too late.

V. OVERLOAD PRINCIPLE

With defensive men assigned to certain areas of the court, it is strategically sound to place more men in an area of the court than can be covered by the man or men assigned to that area. Once there, the movement must not stagnate. It is not enough to be content with one overloaded situation. The two earlier principles continue to apply. If a good percentage shot does not come, the ball and the men should again be moved quickly into another advantage situation for the offense. Obviously, this continues until the goal is achieved. Sometimes the player who occupies this territory will have the best shot if the ball can be moved quickly to him, and he certainly is a key factor on the offensive boards.

VI. CONTINUITY

Since movement is so important, it is necessary to build into the offense a means for continually rotating the men within the patterned attack. Once begun, an offense should have the capacity to continue indefinitely. An option can occur at any time the defensive adjustment forces it, but there should be no need to "set up" again or move players back to their initial positions. You must be cautious not to overemphasize pattern play, because your players may become too pattern conscious at the expense of legitimate offensive opportunities they could create with some personal initiative.

An orderly, step-by-step explanation of all the various offensive possibilities must take place before you can expect the team to make the most of the attack. The reasons for each movement must be clearly understood and practiced until they become habitual.

VII. POST PLAY AGAINST THE ZONE

It is essential that a team continue to threaten the defense with at least one man in the area of a high, medium, or low post. With rapid movement of the ball into different areas of the court, the position of the post man forces continual adjustments in defensive coverage. The post man must be extremely active, alert, and aggressive in establishing his post position.

You may prefer to rotate a new man into the area of the post as the ball is moved around the perimeter. You may also wish to use more than one man at a time in the area of the post. In the first instance, it is difficult for the defense to keep vision on new men flashing to post positions. It also provides movement through the heart of the zone, making it compress momentarily thereby opening up possibilities for good perimeter shots. This must create some confusion on the part of the defense as to whose responsibility the new man becomes and for how long a period of time that responsibility lasts. With two men in the post area, a power game is established, providing the offense with opportunities to pick for one another, get excellent position on the boards, and increase the pressure on the defense inside where one mistake would be very costly.

VIII. PLAYING IN THE SEAMS

Regardless of the initial position taken by a zone, all positions become somewhat similar after the first pass. Usually one defensive man will be covering the ball, one player will have to cover the post man, and one player from the weakside will drop into a position in the lane for rebounding purposes and to defend against movement near the basket. This leaves gaps in the defensive alignment, semi-open positions in those areas where zone coverage by individuals begins and ends. It creates another problem for the defense because the players are not always sure just where responsibility starts and where it ends.

Here is a good example of how the principles work together for the effectiveness of the overall attack. Rapid movement of the ball and the men leads to a spreading of the defense. Placement of a post man adds stress to the inside coverage. Now, playing in the seams of the defense becomes both a possibility and an advantage. It permits penetration of a player with his face to the basket for the purpose of taking a quick shot or to make a quick pass to an inside man when defensive adjustments take place.

IX. PENETRATION

Penetration by the offense further adds to the growing problems of the defense. The strength of a zone lies in its ability to keep a team away from the basket and to force outside shots from poor percentage shooting areas. Every kind of penetration, therefore, works against this strength. Both a man with the ball and a man without the ball can accomplish this goal. Sometimes it becomes possible because of the doubt that exists as to the responsibility for area coverage. For a man without the ball to penetrate and hold a position may not be sound because it violates the principles of moving men, and it solidifies the defensive players in an advantage position around the post man. To penetrate *and move*, however, is sound. When the opportunity does not materialize, a new move can be attempted until an opportunity does materialize. For a man with the ball, his penetration along a seam may lead to an excellent shot, or at least to an open pass when defensive players converge on him.

X. DRIVING AGAINST THE ZONE

The misconception that a drive is not possible against a zone has long existed in basketball. For the simple reason that no one man is assigned to cover another man specifically, a drive *does* become possible. It is never really clear just how far a man's responsibility for coverage extends in a zone when there is movement with the ball. Once the drive begins, does the defensive man continue to follow him all the way? Does he leave his assigned area? And, more importantly, when other defensive players attempt to pick up or converge on the driver, opportunities for the open pass are presented. If a man is alert and has good basketball sense, it's hard to say that he is wrong when he goes to the basket for the simple reason that it creates a great many situations and problems for the defense.

XI. SCREENING IN THE ZONE ATTACK

Another practice not ordinarily associated with play against zones is screening. As with the drive, the screen becomes effective because men do not have specific assignments for coverage of individuals. Therefore, when a drive occurs, the defensive man who picks up can be screened somewhere in the area of his assignment *without* great fear that a jump switch will occur to take away the movement or the opportunity for the quick jump shot. Without the ball there is even less of a probability that a screen will be handled as effectively as it would be in a man-to-man situation, again because players are assigned areas and not men.

XII. PERIMETER SHOOTING AGAINST THE ZONE

As was stated earlier, shooting is the name of the game in a zone attack. Many defenses simply will refuse to spread and allow penetration. They sag deeply and defy teams to beat them from the outside, even though it may be from a comparatively short range. Several things should be considered here: (1) Do you really want to take the shot and face the possibility of giving up the ball if you do not have good outside shooters? The score may not permit you the luxury of making this decision, but it should be considered long before the game takes place. (2) An attempt should be made to get the uncontested shot, if possible. Movement of the ball along with the overload principle will help to achieve this. (3) The shot should be taken by the right person. This necessitates an offensive design that will produce this. (4) The offense should establish a position of board strength inside to at least challenge the defensive team. They must, at least, be made to work hard for the advantage they are trying to gain. To keep all the players outside, no matter how congested it is inside, is an admission of defeat.

XIII. REBOUNDING

An offense should not be run without provisions being made for offensive rebounding balance. Considerable time should be spent explaining and practicing the correct moves to the basket from various positions on the court where a shot might occur. Knowing where the shots are likely to occur gives the man in rebounding position a slight advantage in anticipation.

Aggressiveness is an absolute necessity if the person is going to get to the boards. If he finds a clean rebound or a tip is not possible, he should at least attempt to get a piece of the ball to keep it alive.

XIV. BALANCE AGAINST THE FAST BREAK

Many teams employ the zone defense to give them the opportunity to run. They are in excellent position to rebound and start the break. All zone offenses must have features built into them that provide insurance against this possibility. At least one man should be moving back into a defensive position as soon as the ball leaves the shooter's hands. Nothing is more demoralizing than to spend a great deal of time in disciplined play working for the good percentage shot and then to give up an uncontested lay-up after a lightning-like fast break.

XV. PLAY AGAINST ODD AND EVEN MAN FRONTS

When playing against a standard zone (one that does not match up), a good rule to follow is to establish an opposite alignment from the front line of the zone being attacked. For example, an even front such as a 2-3 or a 2-1-2 would be attacked with a 1-3-1 or a 1-2-2 set. A 1-3-1, 1-2-2, or 3-2 zone would be countered by a 2-1-2 or a 2-3 zone set. This places men *in the gaps* initially and sets up shots from the weak areas of the zone even without movement. It forces immediate defensive adjustment and does not provide the defense with a natural match-up situation.

Adjusting to the odd and even fronts

Most teams have a basic alignment from which they begin most patterns of attack, whether it be man-to-man or zone. It is best for the players to begin from positions with which they are familiar. After they recognize the type of defense they are facing, they can then adjust quickly and without confusion to the style of attack that is to be run against it. If a team remains in a standard zone, this adjustment would not be necessary as the game goes on. The offense could go right into their attack immediately. But at the beginning this probing may be necessary to find out what you are up against.

METHODS OF ADJUSTMENT:

A. Send a guard through after a pass to a guard or forward.

Adjustment from a 2-1-2 alignment to a
1-3-1. (*Diagrams 1-1 and 1-2*)

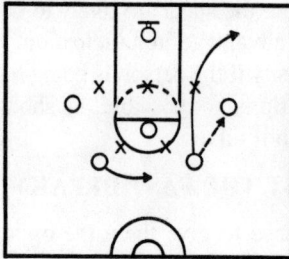

Diagram 1-1

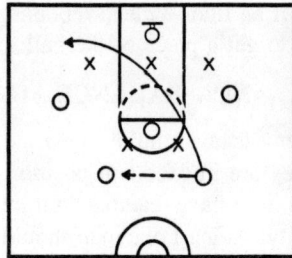

Diagram 1-2

B. Bring a man to the post from the baseline or from the wing.

Adjustment from a 1-2-2 to a 1-3-1.
(*Diagrams 1-3 and 1-4*)

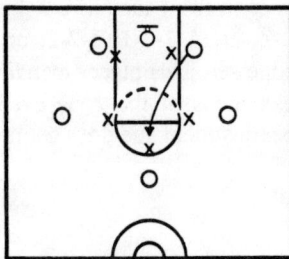

Diagram 1-3

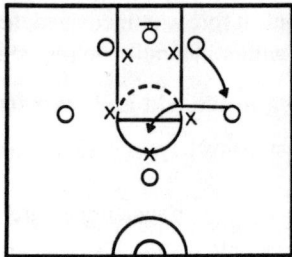

Diagram 1-4

C. Empty areas and fill areas.

Adjustment from 2-1-2 to 1-2-2. (*Diagram 1-5*)

Diagram 1-5

Adjustment from 1-2-2 to 2-1-2. (*Diagram 1-6*)

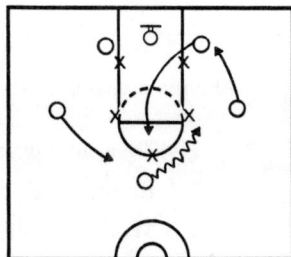

Diagram 1-6

Adjustment from 1-2-2 to 2-2-1. (*Diagram 1-7*)

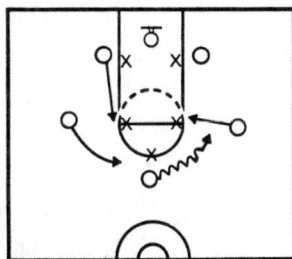

Diagram 1-7

These, of course, only serve as examples of the way adjustments may be accomplished. Each of you will wish to devise your own methods of adjusting to the type of attack you want to run against the different zones and to develop appropriate signals to key the action.

I also recommend that a simple method of checking the type of defense be devised. Sending a guard through will usually accomplish this. Crossing the guards out front or the forwards inside will also achieve the same goal. (*Diagram 1-8*)

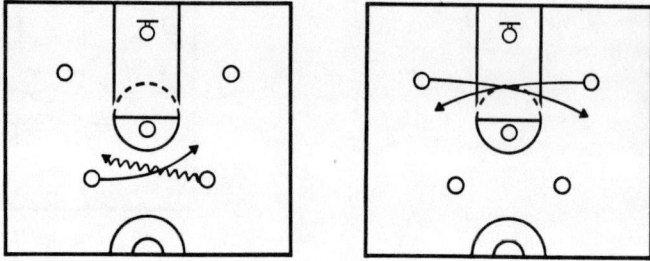

Diagram 1-8

To review, these are the major goals to keep in mind:

1. Take intelligent and good percentage shots.
2. Be prepared to take advantage of every fast break opportunity.
3. Move the ball quickly and with precision.
4. Move men rapidly and with a purpose.
5. Overload areas of the court and look for offensive advantages.
6. Be able to rotate and continue the motion until you get the shot you are looking for.
7. Pressure the defense from past positions.
8. Take advantage of defensive weaknesses in the seams of their alignment.
9. Penetrate the zone.
10. Drive against the zone.
11. Help teammates to free themselves by means of screens.
12. Establish good rebounding balance.
13. Maintain balance against the fast break.
14. Take proper advantage of the odd and even front zones.

SPECIAL NOTE:

Because of the extremely wide variation in zone defenses, rules of operation, coaching philosophies, and styles of play, it is very difficult to provide answers for all conceivable problems that may arise. In my opinion the earlier principles being advocated are essential considerations in the development of any offense designed to attack a team using zone principles.

In the preparation of an attack, many personal preferences exist with regard to such things as player alignment, types of movement, and points of emphasis. Generally speaking, an attack must fit the individual coach's philosophy of play and it must make sense to him.

Therefore, *many* different types of attacks against the short zones are presented in the hope that each of you will be able to find a style that is in keeping with your approach to the game.

Chapter 2

ATTACKING THE ZONES WITH ODD AND EVEN MAN FRONTS

THE ODD MAN FRONTS

The three major types of zones that use odd man fronts are the 1-2-2, the 1-3-1, and the 3-2. The 1-2-2 and the 3-2 zones are almost identical except for the greater coverage by the 3-2 on the sides and the more compressed coverage by the front man on the high post. Whereas the 1-2-2 (or so-called "jug" defense) is tough on the ball as it is moved around the perimeter, the 3-2 is a bit more passive and sagged toward the basket. While a 2-1-2 offense would be good against the 1-2-2 defense, it might not be as effective against the 3-2 because of the position of the middle man in front. The corners and the middle are both susceptible to attack in these two defenses.

The 1-3-1 is very vulnerable to attack in the corners, but strong in the middle. It is also weak in the seams between the point man and the wings. The most effective offenses against this alignment are the 1-2-2, the 2-1-2, and the 2-2-1.

Areas of weakness:

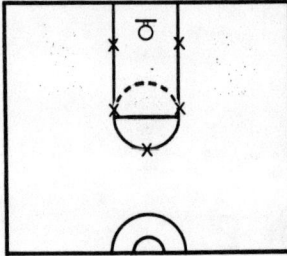

Diagram 2-1

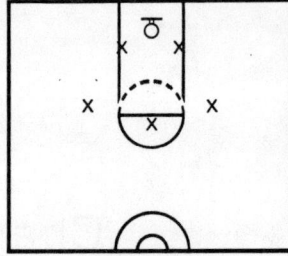

Diagram 2-2

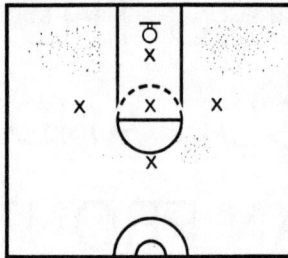

Diagram 2-3

Coverage in the 1-2-2 zone

The areas of individual responsibility are indicated in the diagrams:

For X1 *(Diagram 2-4)*

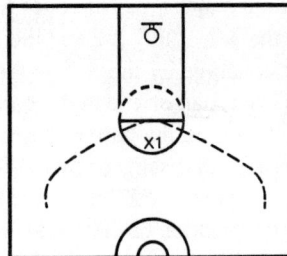

Diagram 2-4

For X2 and X3 *(Diagram 2-5)*

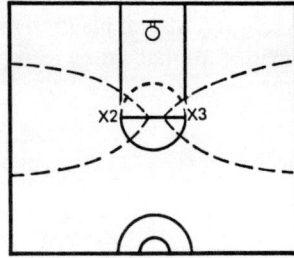

Diagram 2-5

For X4 *(Diagram 2-6)*

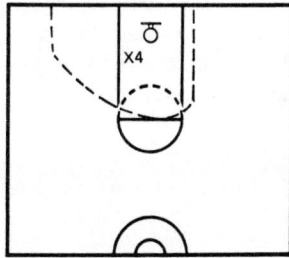

Diagram 2-6

For X5 *(Diagram 2-7)*

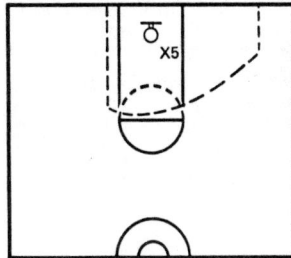

Diagram 2-7

With a man at the high post and only one player near the baseline, a defensive man stationed low will have to come high to cover the man at the post. *(Diagram 2-8)*

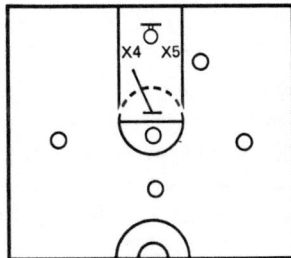

Diagram 2-8

If an offensive wing position is vacated and there is a man at the high post, the defensive man from that side will move over to cover the post. *(Diagram 2-9)*

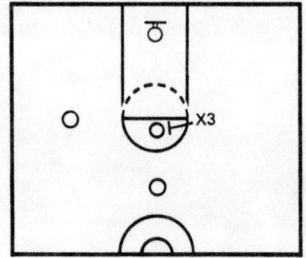

Diagram 2-9

If the ball is passed to the high post, either a bottom man and the point will converge on him while the wing drops back to help cover inside. *(Diagram 2-10)*

(or)

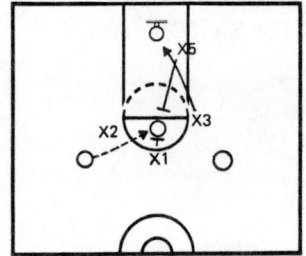

Diagram 2-10

The wing and the point will converge to cover the post man with the ball. *(Diagram 2-11)*

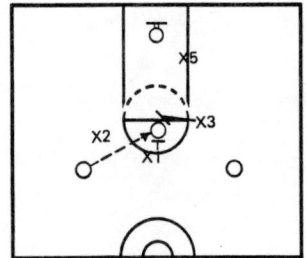

Diagram 2-11

When the ball is moved to the corner, X4 will go out to cover as X5 takes the responsibility for coverage at the low post. X3 drops back to cover low and to take the off-side rebounding responsibility. X2 moves down slightly toward the basket and X1 goes to the top corner of the key on the ball side. *(Diagram 2-12)*

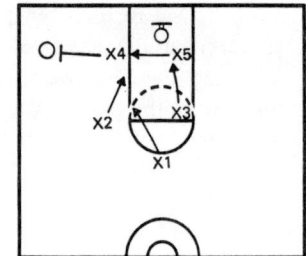

Diagram 2-12

Coverage in the 3-2 zone

The areas of individual responsibility are indicated in the diagrams:

For X1 *(Diagram 2-13)*

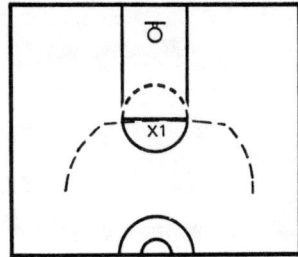

Diagram 2-13

For X2 and X3 *(Diagram 2-14)*

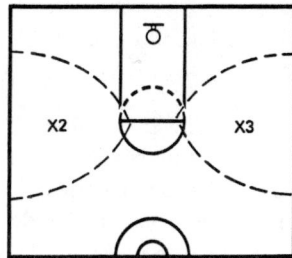

Diagram 2-14

For X4 *(Diagram 2-15)*

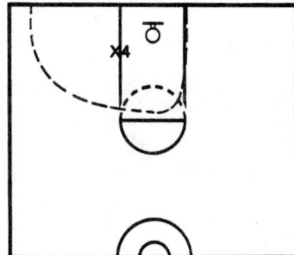

Diagram 2-15

For X5 *(Diagram 2-16)*

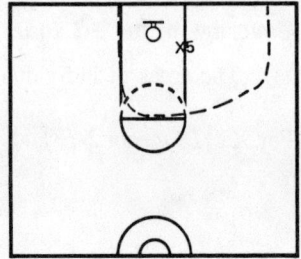

Diagram 2-16

The point man usually makes an effort to front a man at the high post. *(Diagram 2-17)*

Diagram 2-17

If the ball is passed to the high post, usually a bottom man must come up to help cover him because the wing's responsibility keeps him too wide. The wing would then have to drop back to help cover inside. *(Diagram 2-18)*

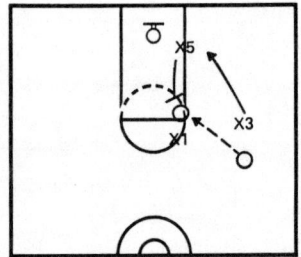

Diagram 2-18

When the ball is moved to the corner, X5 will go out to cover as X4 takes the responsibility for coverage at the low post. X1 will help low or try to prevent a pass to the high post. X2 drops low to take offside rebounding responsibilities. *(Diagram 2-19)*

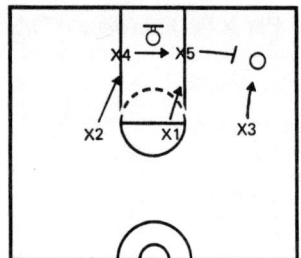

Diagram 2-19

Coverage in the 1-3-1 zone

The areas of individual responsibility are indicated in the diagrams.

For X1 *(Diagram 2-20)*

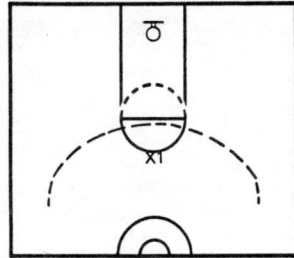

Diagram 2-20

For X2 and X3 *(Diagram 2-21)*

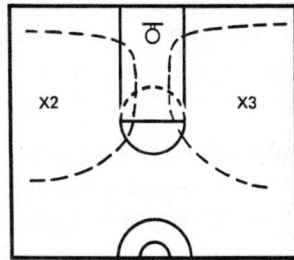

Diagram 2-21

For X4 *(Diagram 2-22)*

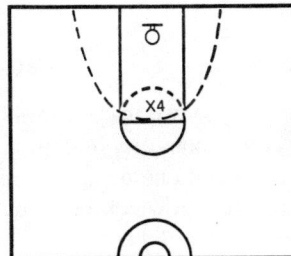

Diagram 2-22

For X5 *(Diagram 2-23)*

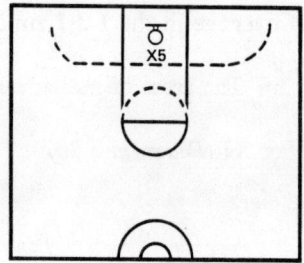

Diagram 2-23

A big problem for the 1-3-1 is the double low post. As X5 commits himself to one of these posts, either X2 or X4 must drop back to help cover inside. Generally, this will be X2 if there is an offensive man at the high post. *(Diagram 2-24)*

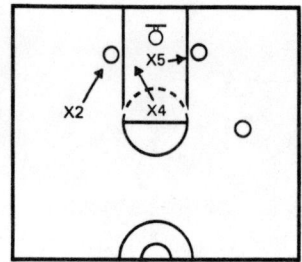

Diagram 2-24

When the ball is in the corner, X5 must take it as X4 drops down to take anyone at the low post. X2 will drop back to take offside rebounding responsibility. *(Diagram 2-25)*

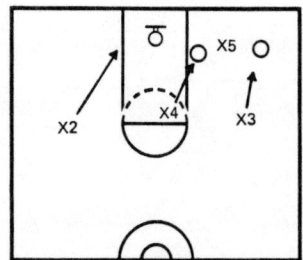

Diagram 2-25

THE EVEN MAN FRONTS

The two major zones that use even man fronts are the 2-1-2 and the 2-3. These zones are, of course, similar, but there are several notable differences, the major one being the different positions taken by the middle man and the distance to which the wing men move out to assume responsibility for wing shots. The 2-1-2 gives greater freedom to the defensive guards to roam out in front since they do not have the responsibility to cover a man at the high post. The 2-3 is the strongest of all the zones under the basket because it has more defensive players in that area. It possesses great rebounding strength and forces most attacks to take outside shots. A 2-1-2 alignment is good against a 2-3, but would be poor against a 2-1-2. The 1-3-1 would be effective against both, but far more so against the 2-3. A 1-2-2 alignment is particularly effective against both.

The 2-3 is vulnerable against good outside shooting and is weak against the man at the pivot. The 2-1-2 is also not terribly effective against wing shots and the corner shot is a threat against this defense. On occasion, the man at the low post can get a shot as the baseline defensive man moves out to cover in the corner.

Areas of weakness:

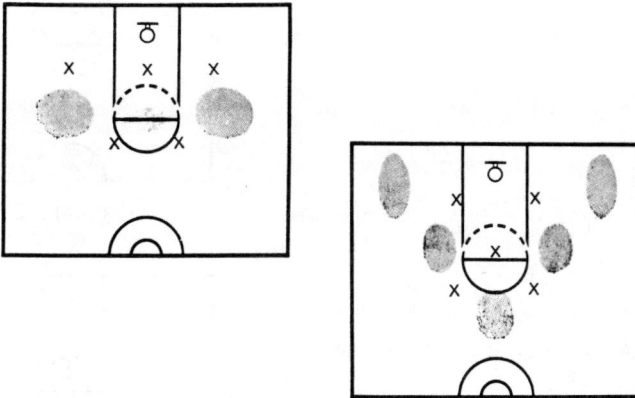

Diagram 2-26

Coverage in the 2-3 zone

The areas of individual responsibility are indicated in the diagrams:

For X1 and X2 *(Diagram 2-27)*

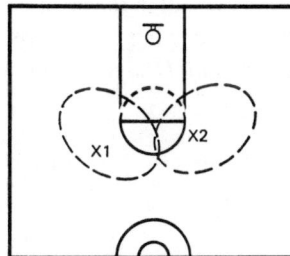

Diagram 2-27

For X3 and X5 *(Diagram 2-28)*

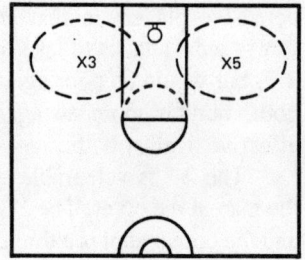

Diagram 2-28

For X4 *(Diagram 2-29)*

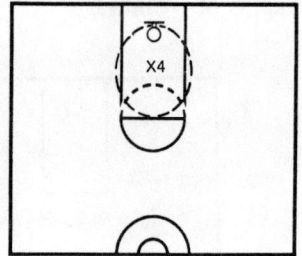

Diagram 2-29

With a man at the high post and two guards out front, the man in the middle will have to come high to cover the man at the post. *(Diagram 2-30)*

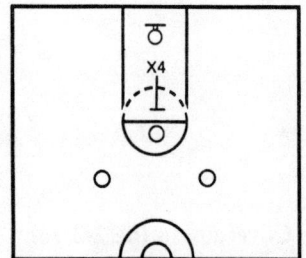

Diagram 2-30

With the ball in the hands of a wing man, the defensive wing will have to come out to cover him. *(Diagram 2-31)*

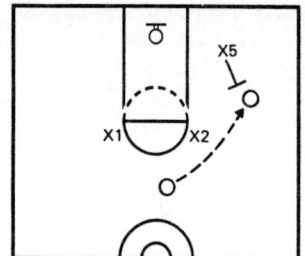

Diagram 2-31

When the ball is in the corner, a defensive wing will have to move out to cover it while X4 takes the responsibility for the low post. *(Diagram 2-32)*

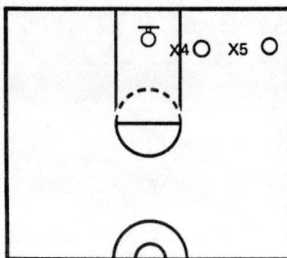

Diagram 2-32

Coverage in the 2-1-2 zone

The areas of individual responsibility are indicated in the diagrams:

For X1 and X2 *(Diagram 2-33)*

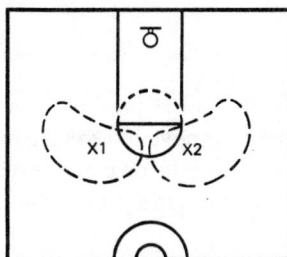

Diagram 2-33

For X4 *(Diagram 2-34)*

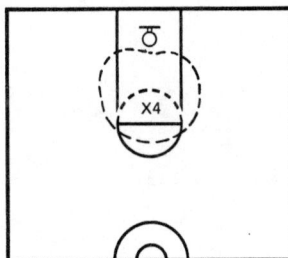

Diagram 2-34

For X3 and X5 *(Diagram 2-35)*

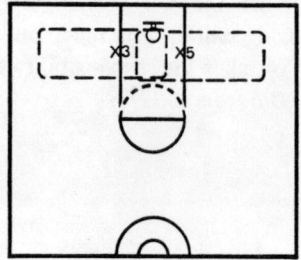

Diagram 2-35

If the ball is passed to a wing deeper than the defensive guard on that side, a baseline defensive man may have to come out to cover him. *(Diagram 2-36)*

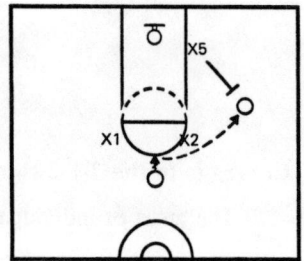

Diagram 2-36

If the ball is passed to the corner, X5 will have to move out to take him and X4 *or* X3 will have to take the responsibility for the low post. *(Diagram 2-37)*

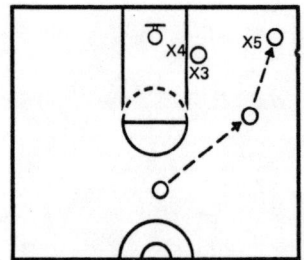

Diagram 2-37

Chapter 3

DEVELOPING THE IMPORTANT INDIVIDUAL TECHNIQUES

You should clearly instruct your players in the individual techniques and methods of play within the zone attack. Merely pointing out *where* a player should go within a motion is not enough; he must be taught *how* to execute the many little things that make an attack successful.

INDIVIDUAL CUTS FROM THE STRONGSIDE AND FROM THE WEAKSIDE

Individual cuts from the strongside or from the weakside should make use of misdirection. By misdirection is meant an initial move away from the spot where the player hopes to receive the ball. The zone defense is geared to strong ballside defense, and zone defenders have a good idea where the cuts will be made. Still, the defenders have to respect a change of pace, a fake, or a change of direction. *(Diagram 3-1)*

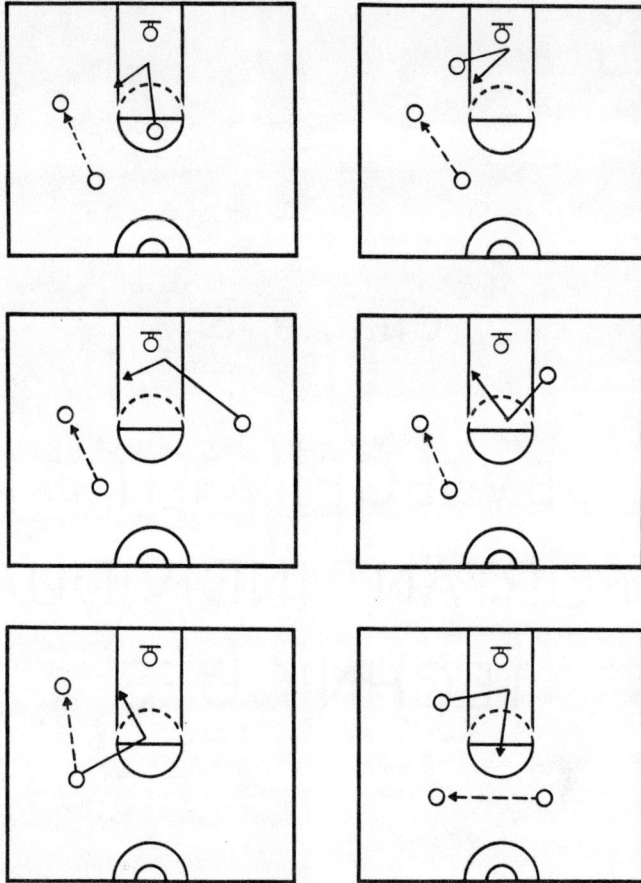

Diagram 3-1

Examples:

Baseline cuts tend to compress the defense because they must respect a threat to the basket. The natural tendency is to make a defensive move to counter the threat. Moves away from the basket are most generally "eyeballed" in zone as well as in man-to-man situations. Compressing or flattening a zone can result in closer shots. It also makes it difficult for the defense to help up the middle or at the top of the key.

Triangulation moves and baseline cuts must be practiced often and rein-
forced regularly. You should demand that your players make precise stops and
turns, and even go so far as marking the routes they are to follow with tape
during practice. In triangular moves, the receiver cuts toward the basket,
taking the defender 2 or 3 steps, cuts at a 90 degree angle away from his
original direction, and then returns for a pass with the defender blocked off at
his hip. *(Diagram 3-2)* Some purists require the step across be a reverse turn,
but any effective cross-step should suffice.

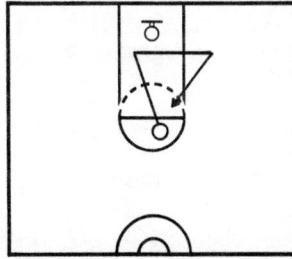

Diagram 3-2

When coming to meet the pass, the offensive man should not split the
defenders evenly because he then gives each an opportunity to intercept or
deflect the pass. *(Diagram 3-3)*

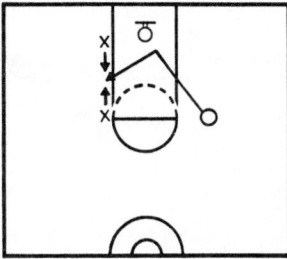

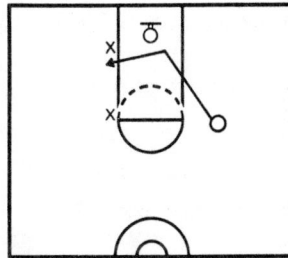

Diagram 3-3

Instead, he should make contact with a defensive man, get the near foot
slightly ahead of the defensive man if possible, and control him with the near
hip and elbow as he provides a target with his free arm and hand. *(Diagram
3-4)*

Diagram 3-4

Gaining advantage position

When speaking of "advantage position" inside, we are referring to a position held by the low post that enables him to beat the defensive player assigned to cover him. Essentially, there are four positions in which the low post may find himself:

A. *Defensive man behind the low post* **(Advantage)** Taking into account the skills of today's players, a defensive man cannot play directly behind a man at the low post and consistently stop him from scoring. Almost *anyone* who receives the ball at the low post has a decent chance of getting off a quick shot or of drawing the foul if he has mastered the muscle shot. More on this later. *(Diagram 3-5)*

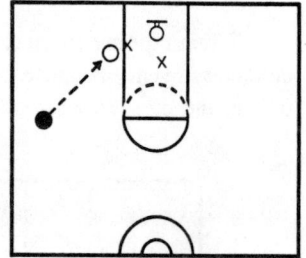

Diagram 3-5

B. *Defensive man in top side-front position* **(Advantage)** The offensive man can now shut out the defensive man with his near hip and elbow and receive a pass on the baseline side where there is no defensive help. *(Diagram 3-6)*

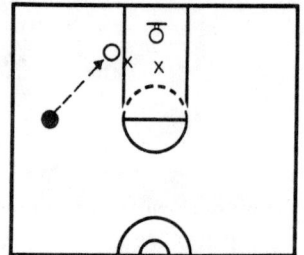

Diagram 3-6

C. *Defensive man on baseline side-front position* (**Probable disadvantage**) In most cases this is a strong defensive position because a pass would have to be thrown into the middle of the lane where there is defensive help. *(Diagram 3-7)*

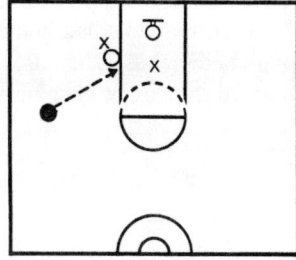

Diagram 3-7

D. *Defensive man in dead front position on the low post* (**Probable disadvantage**) Two factors are of great importance here: (1) Height of the offensive player at the low post and (2) weakside help. With truly superior height and an absence of weakside help, this would be an advantage position for the offense; in most zone alignments, however, the coverage is such that the offense has little opportunity to gain an advantage. *(Diagram 3-8)*

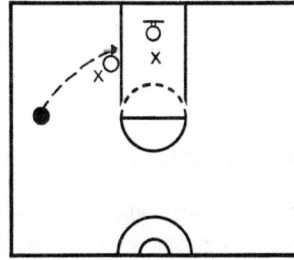

Diagram 3-8

It is necessary to drill low post men and those in a position to feed them to help both learn to immediately recognize advantage position when they see it. It is essential that the player at the low post indicate his advantage by raising a target hand as he fends off the defensive player with the other elbow. There are many good drills to accomplish this goal, but what really needs to be practiced in each are the adjustments to the ever-changing position of the defensive man.

Muscle shot

Once the ball has penetrated the zone, it is very likely that the defensive men will collapse, surrounding the player in possession and making a finesse shot difficult. The man at the low post, having gained an advantage position, should learn to get off an immediate shot after receiving a pass from a teammate. No finesse is involved in this muscle shot (such as hooking an opponent, showing the ball in one direction while drop-stepping in the other, using a variety of fakes to get the opponent in the air, stepping away from the basket for a sweeping hook shot, etc.)—just a quick release, fully protecting the ball with the lead elbow in the direction of the basket. For example, if a right-handed player receives the pass on the left side (with his back to the basket), he immediately makes a quarter turn to his left, firmly grips the ball with both hands as he raises it to his eye-level, points his left elbow straight up toward the basket keeping the forearm parallel to the floor, and goes straight toward the basket to release it with the right hand. *(Diagram 3-9)*

Diagram 3-9

On the other side, his lead arm would be his right, using his right elbow to protect the ball. *(Diagram 3-10)*

Diagram 3-10

The elbow should not be used as a weapon, but the ball must be protected and this is an excellent method of protecting it. If contact with the defensive man occurs while the shooter is moving *up toward the basket* on his shot, the foul will probably be defensive. Occasionally an offensive foul may be called, but with all the objectives being sought, it must be considered a "good" foul.

Penetrate and pass off

Perhaps the simplest and quickest means of compressing an area of the zone is penetration by a man with the ball. Finding gaps and penetrating them is a major objective in all zone attacks. Players need to be schooled in the techniques of getting the ball to the open man when the gap is closed. The first principle they must understand is: *pass to the side from which you get pressure*. Hopefully, both men will be attracted to the ball on the attempted penetration. If this happens, a pass to both sides is available. If only one defensive man collapses, however, the pass should be made to that player's side. *(Diagram 3-11)* A second principle: *make the good pass to the open man*. This probably sounds ridiculously simple, but it is the key to clear shots against the zone and, therefore, is of tremendous importance to the coach in his work with individuals. If, for example, the collapsing defensive man comes at the penetrating offensive player with his hands up, the pass should be a bounce pass. And, of course, the opposite is also true: the ball should be passed over the top of a man who has his hands down. The man with the ball must be trained to use his peripheral vision fully. He cannot allow the defensive maneuver to disconcert him and ruin his vision. He must *see* his teammate, and make the accurate pass to set him up for the quick shot.

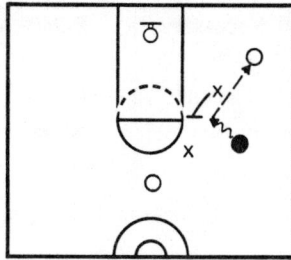

Diagram 3-11

SPECIAL NOTE:

Several attacks are offered against each of the various zone alignments. This by no means limits the effectiveness of any of these motions to that one defense. They are merely illustrated combating a defense against which I feel they might be most effective. The final decision is up to you.

Accompanying each attack is a checklist of important factors to be considered when selecting the offense. These are, (1) Man and ball movement, (2) Outside shooting, (3) Tempo of attackers, (4) Low post action, and (5) Size.

The first item considers the extent to which the players move within the attack and how much the ball needs to be passed around before a good shot is earned. On the chart, the range of man and ball movement extends from "considerable" to "limited."

In outside shooting an attempt is made to indicate the degree to which a team needs to depend on the perimeter shot to make the offense work.

Timing in the cuts and passes is an important ingredient of any patterned attack. Most zone offenses establish a team cadence, ranging from quick hitting and rapid movement to those that need to develop slowly, with the mean rate being normal or half-speed. The players need to know if the attack is intended to give the defense time to react and then exploit that reaction or to attack with quickness by whipping the ball in and out as well as around the perimeter.

How much does the attack stress low post play? Does it depend on this action to have maximum success or is it an insignificant feature? The range extends from stressed to unstressed.

If the size of the players is a major role in the success of the motion, it is suggested on the chart, ranging from "Big man needed" to "Size not a major factor."

Man and Ball Movement	Outside Shooting	Tempo of Attackers	Low Post Action	Size
Considerable	Necessary	Rapid	Stressed	Big men
Normal	Normal	Normal	Normal	Normal
Limited	Unstressed	Slow	Unstressed	Not major factor

Chapter 4

DEFEATING THE 1-2-2 ZONE DEFENSE

ATTACKING A 1-2-2 ZONE FROM A 1-2-2 ALIGNMENT

Attack number 1

Man and Ball Movement	Outside Shooting	Tempo of Attackers	Low Post Action	Size
Normal	Normal	Normal	Stressed	Normal

The two low men take a tandem set on one side near the baseline. 1 passes the ball to 2 on the strong side. As this pass is made, 5 turns and *picks* for 4 who steps out looking for a pass from 2. We can assume that X5 will cross the lane to help in this situation. *(Diagram 4-1)*

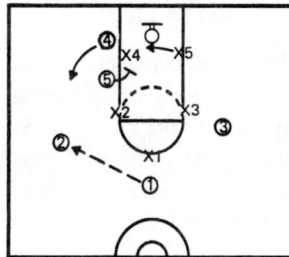

Diagram 4-1

As soon as 2 receives the pass, he tries to *split the seam* between X2 and X1 on a dribble. The idea here is to draw the two men to him. This will lead to a numbers advantage elsewhere. As this is happening, 3 drops down to the basket looking for a pass from 2. 1 fills 3's vacated spot on the off-ball side. 2 should keep his eye on X3 to see how he covers the two men. If he drops down to cover 3, then 1 should be open. If he does not cover him, 3 should be open for a lob pass right at the basket and an easy shot. *(Diagram 4-2)*

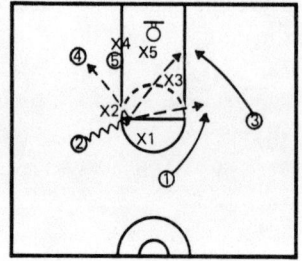

Diagram 4-2

Great stress is put on X4—if he goes around 5 to try and cover 4, 2 can throw the ball directly to 5 at the basket. *(Diagram 4-3)*

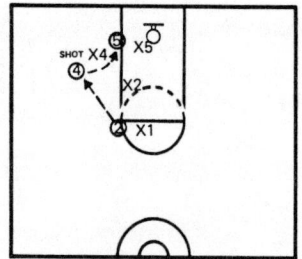

Diagram 4-3

ROTATION

If the ball is passed to 1, he may have a *good percentage shot* immediately. 3 will move quickly to the corner as 5 crosses the lane to a low *post* position. A pass to 3 may lead to a *good percentage shot* from the short corner. *(Diagram 4-4)*

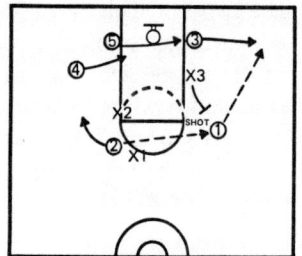

Diagram 4-4

The same opportunities are again available. 1 should try to split the seam between X1 and X3. This again puts great stress on the coverage near the baseline and 1 should look for all four pass possibilities in the same manner as before. *(Diagram 4-5)*

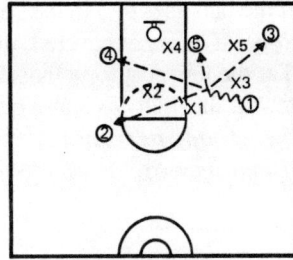

Diagram 4-5

Attack number 2

Man and Ball Movement	Outside Shooting	Tempo of Attackers	Low Post Action	Size
Considerable	Necessary	Rapid	Stressed	Normal

In this offense, the wing on the weakside (3) drops a little lower toward the baseline than the wing (2) on the strong side. 4 and 5 take tandem *post* positions near the baseline. 1 may pass to 2 to start the motion or occasionally to 3, who steps up quickly to a high *post* on the weak side. If 1 passes to 3, he should follow the pass and look for a return pass and a shot behind the *screen* set by 3. *(Diagram 4-6)*

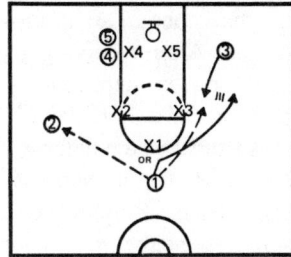

Diagram 4-6

If 1 passes to 2, 4 splits away from the tandem post and comes to a mid-*post* position part way up the lane. 3 crosses over into the corner on the ball side. 2 can hit either 3, 4, or 5. *(Diagram 4-7)*

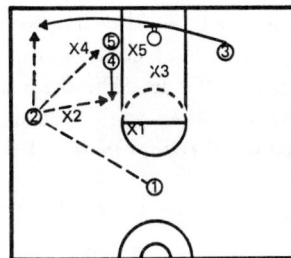

Diagram 4-7

If the ball goes to 3 in the corner, he can take a shot if he is not covered, dump the ball into 5 at the low post for a muscle shot, or pass it to 4 at the high *post* for a quick jump *shot at the good percentage shooting area. (Diagram 4-8)*

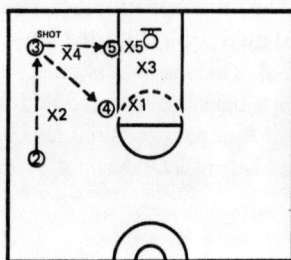

Diagram 4-8

ROTATION

If none of this goes, 3 will pass back out to 2. 2 then swings it to 1 and hurries to the wing on the other side. 3 moves to the other corner. After receiving the pass, 1 drives hard for a few steps looking for an advantage position and a shot. 4 and 5 hold, expecting a pass from 1 as the defense slides to the other side with the movement of the ball. By watching the flow of the defense, 1 may be able to see either 4 or 5 come open momentarily for a quick pass. *(Diagram 4-9)*

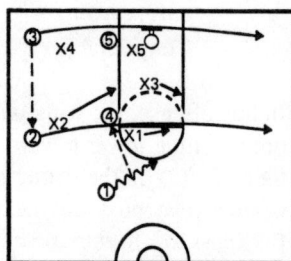

Diagram 4-9

1 passes to 2. After the pass, 4 flashes to the low *post* and 5 comes to the high post. These men should read the defense and come into the area at an angle that takes advantage of the *gaps*. *(Diagram 4-10)*

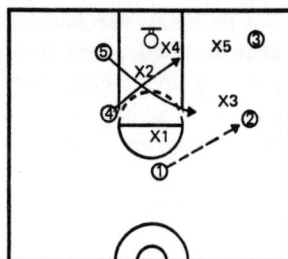

Diagram 4-10

2 may now hit any one of these men and look for situations as previously described on the other side of the court. *(Diagram 4-11)*

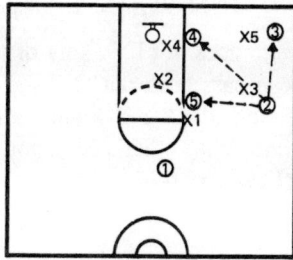

Diagram 4-11

Attack number 3

Man and Ball Movement	Outside Shooting	Tempo of Attackers	Low post Action	Size
Normal	Normal	Normal	Stressed	Big men

1 starts the offense by passing to a wing on either side and then cutting down the lane and around the low post on the ball side looking for a return pass and a quick *good percentage shot*. The other wing (2) flashes to the high *post* on the ball side right behind 1's cut down the lane. 3 should begin a quick dribble away from his intended pass to move the defenses. *(Diagram 4-12)*

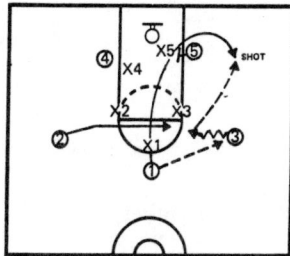

Diagram 4-12

If the ball is passed to 1, he may also dump the ball into 5 at the low *post* or pass it back out to 2 at the high *post*.

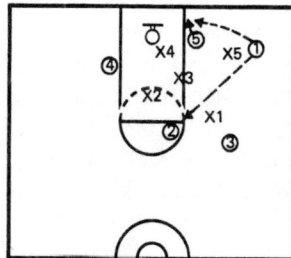

Diagram 4-13

ROTATION

If 1 does not have any of these options, he can pass back out to 3 and move across the lane under 5 and 4 and out to the wing position on the other side. 2 pops out to the point. *(Diagram 4-14)*

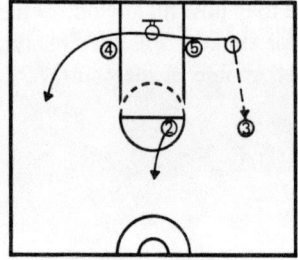

Diagram 4-14

Now the ball is passed to 2 at the point. He then hits the wing (1) on the other side and cuts down the lane and around the low post on the ball side looking for a return pass as 3 flashes to the high *post*. To keep the defense honest, the wings should constantly look to get the ball directly inside to the low *post* on their side. *(Diagram 4-15)*

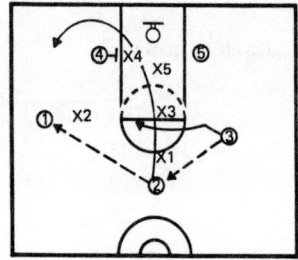

Diagram 4-15

Attack number 4

Man and Ball Movement	Outside Shooting	Tempo of Attackers	Low post Action	Size
Normal	Necessary	Rapid	Normal	Normal

In this motion, the offense is looking to get *good percentage shots* from behind screens as the ball is moved rapidly around the perimeter. The point man (1) passes to a wing (3). As this happens, 5 goes away from the ball, under 4's *screen*, and out to a deep wing spot. 2 also *picks* down on the defensive wing, helping to provide a double *screen* for 5. *(Diagram 4-16)*

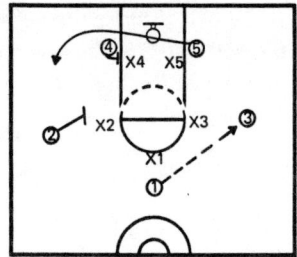

Diagram 4-16

The ball is passed back to 1 and moved quickly to 5 for his shot behind the double screen before the zone can shift and recover. Both 2 and 4 may *post* looking to receive a pass from 5 if they have advantage positions on their man. *(Diagram 4-17)*

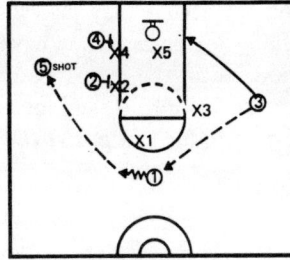

Diagram 4-17

If none of this goes, the ball is passed back to the point man, and 4 moves across the lane under 3's *screen* and out to a deep wing position, looking for a pass and a quick jump shot. 5 drops down to take the low post on the off-ball side to be in good *rebounding* position. *(Diagram 4-18)*

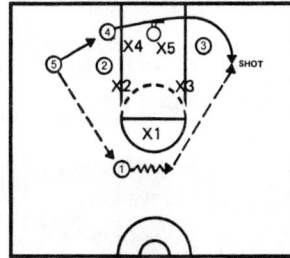

Diagram 4-18

If no shot occurs, it should be swung quickly to the other side with 3 going under the double screen set by 5 and 3. *(Diagram 4-19)*

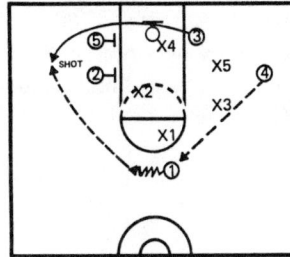

Diagram 4-19

This may continue until a shot occurs. *(Diagram 4-20)*

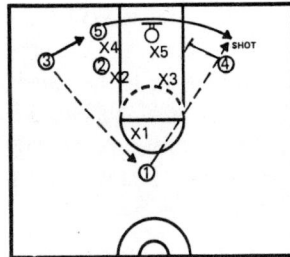

Diagram 4-20

At any time 1 may pass the ball directly to the inside posts if they have advantage position. Also, the men who receive the ball at the deep wings should look to dump the ball inside to the low *posts*. *(Diagram 4-21)*

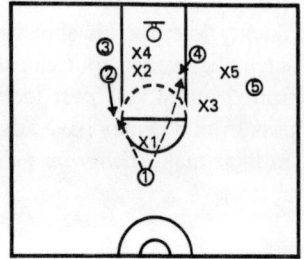

Diagram 4-21

Attack number 5

Man and Ball Movement	Outside Shooting	Tempo of Attackers	Low post Action	Size
Normal	Normal	Rapid	Normal	Normal

The point man (1) passes to a wing (3) and cuts down the lane and under the low post on the off-ball side. 2 follows his move closely, breaking into the middle of the zone expecting a quick pass and a *good percentage shot*. *(Diagram 4-22)*

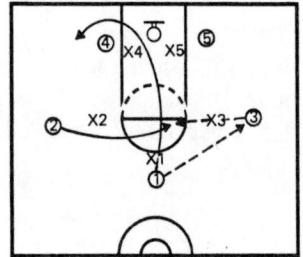

Diagram 4-22

If 2 does not receive the pass, he continues across the court to the other wing position as 3 dribbles out to the point. As this is happening, 4 is breaking into the opening from his low post position expecting a pass for a quick jump shot. 1 moves out to a wing position *(Diagram 4-23)*

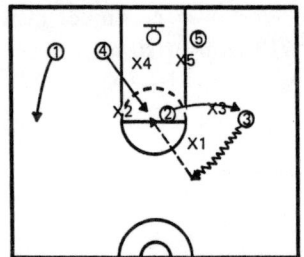

Diagram 4-23

If 3 cannot hit 4 in the middle, he passes to 1 at the wing and 4 and 5 rotate, exchanging their original low post positions. *(Diagram 4-24)*

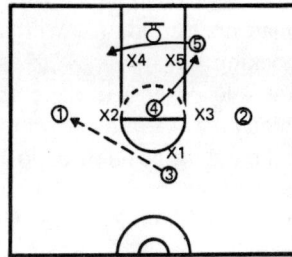

Diagram 4-24

ROTATION

Now the same thing happens again. 3 passes to 1 and cuts down the lane and under 4 at the low post on the off-ball side. 2 flashes into the opening in the middle of the zone looking for a pass. *(Diagram 4-25)*

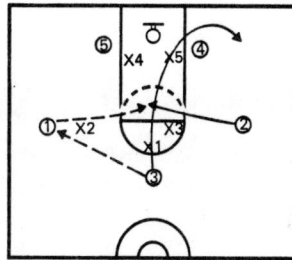

Diagram 4-25

Attack number 6

Man and Ball Movement	Outside Shooting	Tempo of Attackers	Low Post Action	Size
Considerable	Normal	Normal	Stressed	Normal

In this 1-2-2 attack, the wing men and the low post men are inverted. 2 and 3 take positions in the corners while 4 and 5 come up to high *posts*. This should give the point man four pass possibilities to begin the attack. *(Diagram 4-26)*

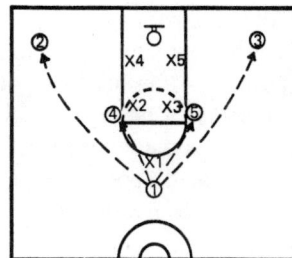

Diagram 4-26

If 1 passes into the corner (3), the high post
man on his side (5) will roll to the basket
looking for a pass as X5 is forced to move
out and cover 3 in the corner. The off-side
high *post* (4), rolls down to take an off-side
rebounding position or to be in position to
take a pass from 5 if X4 moves over to prevent 5's shot. 2 comes from the opposite
corner to a *gap* position in the lane, and 1
moves to the side and opens himself up for a
pass from 3. *(Diagram 4-27)*

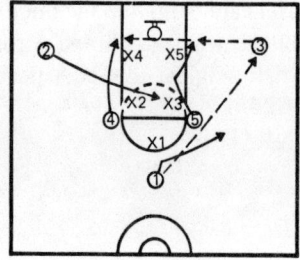

Diagram 4-27

3 may hit 2 in the *gap* for a quick shot or
back the ball out to 1. *(Diagram 4-28)*

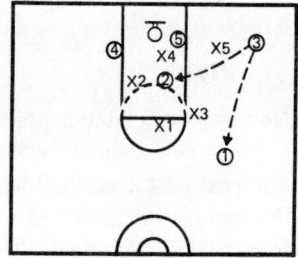

Diagram 4-28

ROTATION

As the ball is being passed out to 1, 5 crosses
the lane to a low *post* position, 2 drops down
to a low *post* on the other side, and 4 comes
straight outside to take a pass from 1.
(Diagram 4-29)

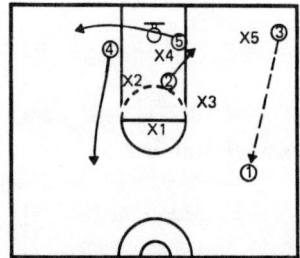

Diagram 4-29

After 1's pass to 4, 4 passes to 5 who has
stepped out into the corner from his low post
position. After his pass, 4 cuts to the basket
expecting a return pass. 3 comes from the
off-side corner into the *gap* in the lane. 1 fills
4's vacated spot in preparation for a pass
from 5. *(Diagram 4-30)*

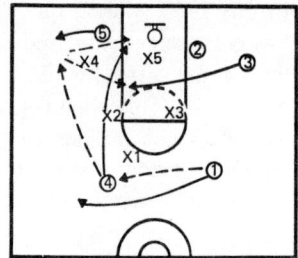

Diagram 4-30

If the first pass goes to a high post (5), he immediately turns and faces the basket. If he is not covered, he can take the *good percentage shot*. 4 cuts diagonally across the lane to a low *post* and 2 moves in from the corner. 5 now has 3 men along the baseline to hit and he simply looks to see who is open. *(Diagram 4-31)*

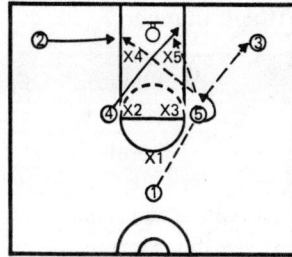

Diagram 4-31

ATTACKING A 1-2-2 ZONE FROM A 1-3-1 ALIGNMENT

Attack number 1

Man and Ball Movement	Outside Shooting	Tempo of Attackers	Low Post Action	Size
Limited	Unstressed	Normal	Stressed	Normal

This motion places great stress on the back two men to cover three offensive players near the basket. The point man (1) dribbles to one side forcing the defensive wing on that side (X3) to come up and stop him along with X1. As this is happening, 3 drops down to a spot near the baseline and about 8-10 feet from the corner. 5 also times a roll to the basket after 1 begins his dribble to give him a target at the basket. 1 now watches the action of X5. If he stays to cover 5, 3 will be open for a pass and a possible quick *good percentage shot*. If X5 steps out to cover 3 in the corner, 5 may be open at the basket for a muscle shot. *Also*, if 1 is very alert, he may notice that X4 comes across to help X5 cover both 5 and 3. This might leave 4 open for a *direct pass at the basket. (Diagram 4-32)*

If 1 cannot hit anyone on this side, he passes across court to 2 who then has the same situation as described on the other side. This may continue until a man is open for the pass and shot. *(Diagram 4-33)*

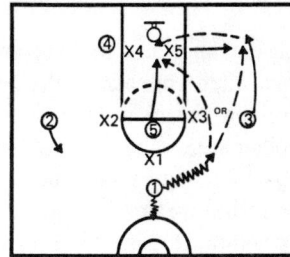

Diagram 4-32

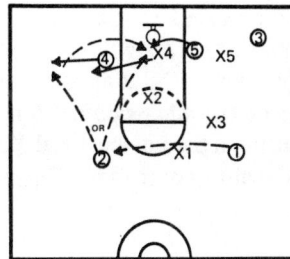

Diagram 4-33

Attack number 7

Man and Ball Movement	Outside Shooting	Temp of Attackers	Low Post Action	Size
Normal	Normal	Normal	Stressed	Normal

The point man (1) starts by passing to a wing (3). As this happens, 4 *screens* down on X5 and 5 rolls down the lane and out under 4's screen looking for a quick pass and a jump shot in a *good percentage shooting area*. *(Diagram 4-34)*

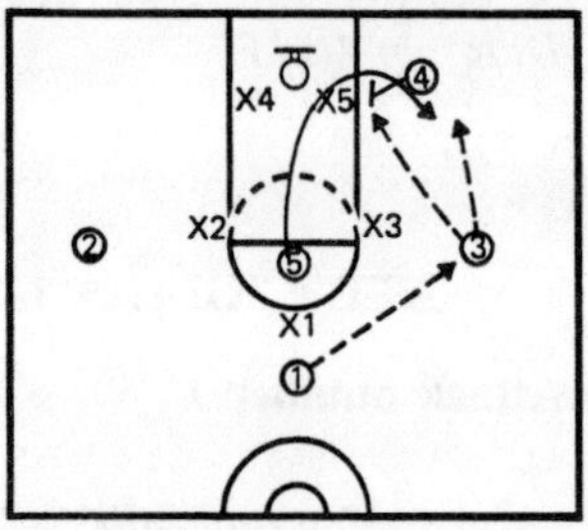

Diagram 4-34

If 3 cannot pass to 5, he swings it back to 1 and then cuts across the lane and under 4's screen out to a deep wing position on the other side. 4 has moved across to a low *post* position and 5 takes a position at the low post on the weak side to be in *rebounding* position. 1 passes the ball to 2. *(Diagram 4-35)*

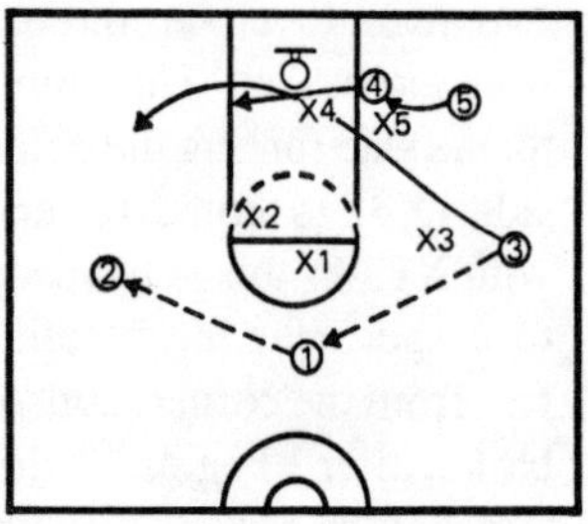

Diagram 4-35

2 now has several pass possibilities: to 3 under the *screen* for a jump shot; to 4 at the low *post* if he is in an advantage position; to 5 on the other side if X5 has come across to help on the low post and X3 has not dropped down to cover him. *(Diagram 4-36)*

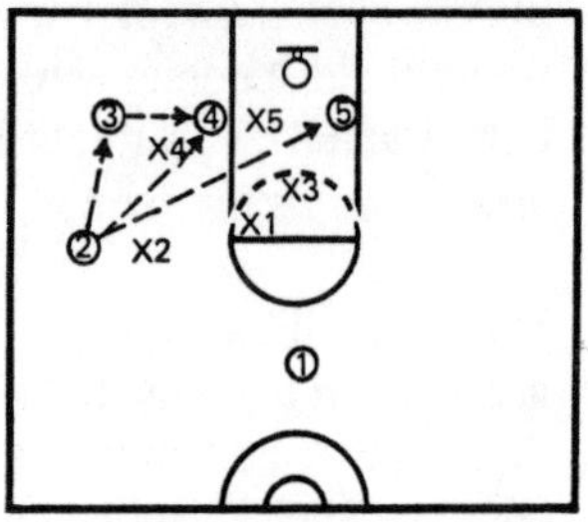

Diagram 4-36

ROTATION

As before, the ball is swung back to the point man and over to 5 stepping out to the wing spot on that side. *(Diagram 4-37)*

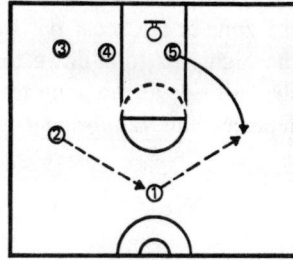

Diagram 4-37

4 comes across to the low *post* on the strong side and 2 cuts under his *screen* after his pass to 1. 3 takes offside *rebounding* position. *(Diagram 4-38)*

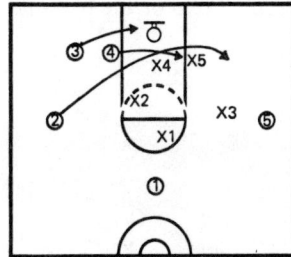

Diagram 4-38

Now the same opportunities exist again, and the motion would continue until a shot is taken. *(Diagram 4-39)*

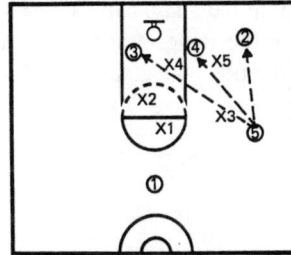

Diagram 4-39

ATTACKING A 1-2-2 ZONE FROM A 2-1-2 ALIGNMENT

Attack number 1

Man and Ball Movement	Outside Shooting	Tempo of Attackers	Low Post Action	Size
Limited	Normal	Slow	Stressed	Normal

The guard with the ball attempts to *penetrate* the zone *at the seam* out front. The man at the high *post* rolls down to the baseline on the ball side as the wing from the other side replaces him. *(Diagram 4-40)*

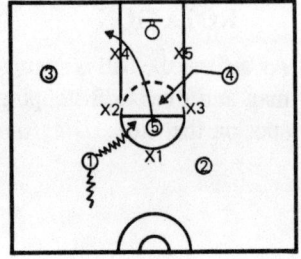

Diagram 4-40

The *movement of the* men now has provided an *overload* on the ball side. *(Diagram 4-41)*

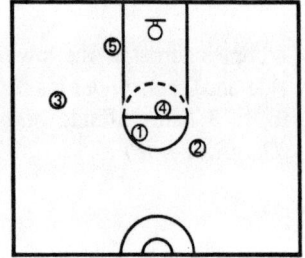

Diagram 4-41

By *driving* at the wing, the guard is forcing him to cover him. When the wing comes to him the guard can pass to 5 at the low post, 3 at the wing, 4 at the new high post, or 2 at the opposite guard position. *(Diagram 4-42)*

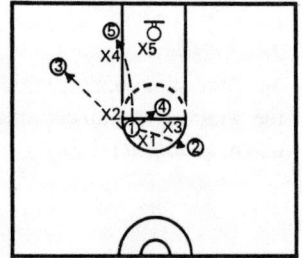

Diagram 4-42

If the ball is passed to 5 at the low post, 3 and 4 *crash the boards* to give the offense a 3 on 2 advantage inside. Guards 1 and 2 move back into a defensive position against the fast break. *(Diagram 4-43)*

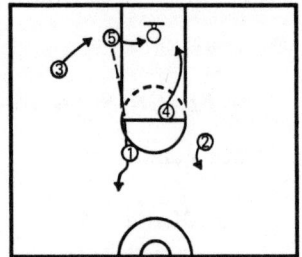

Diagram 4-43

If the ball is passed to 3 at the wing, he looks for an immediate shot. If he is not open, he looks inside to hit 5 at the low *post* or 4 who has come to the new high *post*. *(Diagram 4-44)*

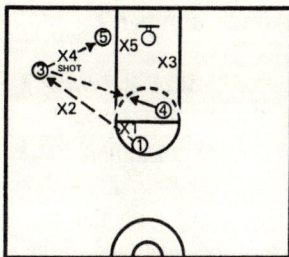

Diagram 4-44

A pass to 4 leads to a quick *drive* to the basket or a jump shot. He may also hit 5 at the low post or 3 at the wing. 1 and 2 are still back against the break. *(Diagram 4-45)*

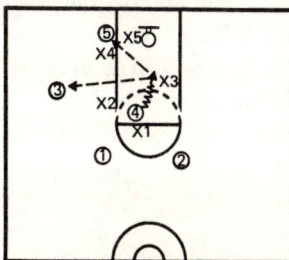

Diagram 4-45

ROTATION

If nothing develops, the ball comes back out to guard 1 who passes across to guard 2. 4 slides to the high post and then down to a low post position. 5 comes out to the wing spot on the ball side as 3 is moving to the strong side high post. *(Diagram 4-46)*

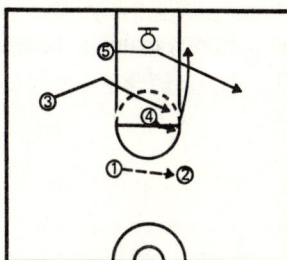

Diagram 4-46

The attack now begins again. 2 attempts to *penetrate* from out front. *(Diagram 4-47)*

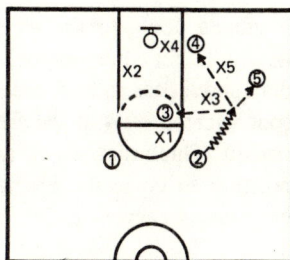

Diagram 4-47

Attack number 2

Man and Ball Movement	Outside Shooting	Tempo of Attackers	Low Post Action	Size
Limited	Normal	Normal	Stressed	Normal

The guard with the ball (1) dribbles away from the seam and to the side in an effort to pull the defensive wing man out on him. As this is happening, 3 steps out to the corner hoping to pull out the low defensive man on his side. At the same time, 5 rolls down to the low *post*. The *overload* has been established. *(Diagram 4-48)*

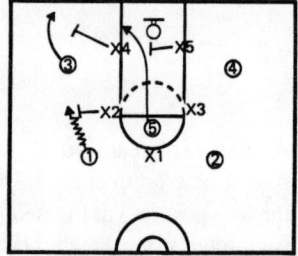

Diagram 4-48

The pass from 1 can go to either 3 or 5, depending upon the play of X4. If it goes to 3, he may have a good shot or at least an opportunity to dump the ball inside to 5 at the low *post*. *(Diagram 4-49)*

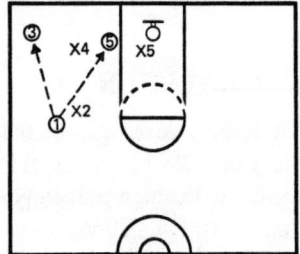

Diagram 4-49

4 moves down to the weak side low *post* hoping to get a position behind the defensive man and a pass right at the basket. 2 fills the spot vacated by 4 at the free-throw line extended. Three men (3, 5, and 4) are now in position to go to the *boards* while 1 and 2 have *break responsibility*. *(Diagram 4-50)*

Diagram 4-50

ROTATION

If the ball is passed to 2, 4 goes to the corner
as 5 fills his spot at the low *post*. 3 fills in at
the off-side low *post* looking for a pass at the
basket and 1 slides down to a wing position.
This can continue until the defense is unable
to adjust to the *overload* and a shot results.
(Diagram 4-51)

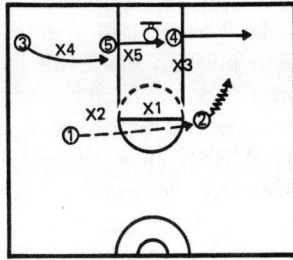

Diagram 4-51

The players are making continual use of a
numbers advantage at the baseline. An offensive triangle is maintained on both sides.
(Diagram 4-52)

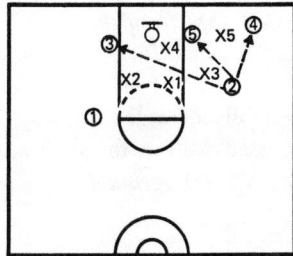

Diagram 4-52

Attack number 3

Man and Ball Movement	Outside Shooting	Tempo of Attackers	Low Post Action	Size
Considerable	Necessary	Rapid	Normal	Not major factor

An attack that emphasizes rapid *movement of
the ball and the men:* 1 passes to 3 and goes
around him into the corner. 2 clears himself
and receives a pass from 3. *(Diagram 4-53)*

Diagram 4-53

The ball is now swung quickly to the other side. 2 passes to 4. 5 drops down into a low *post* position and 3 fills for him at the high *post*. 1 comes from behind the defense along the baseline to the strong side corner. This establishes an *overload* advantage and fits men into the *seams*. *(Diagram 4-54)*

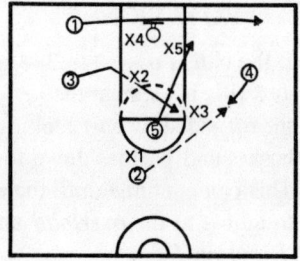

Diagram 4-54

4 may be momentarily uncovered. If so, he should attempt to penetrate and look for the *good shot from the perimeter*. He must always watch for the opportunity to dump the ball into 5 if an advantage position can be established at the low *post*. The ball may be passed to 3 at the high *post* or to 1 in the corner. *(Diagram 4-55)*

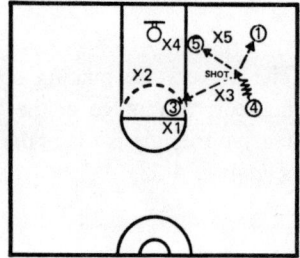

Diagram 4-55

If the ball goes to 3, 1 slides quickly across the lane and to the low *post* on the other side. 4 moves down to a position near the baseline. *(Diagram 4-56)*

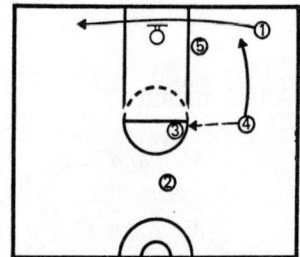

Diagram 4-56

Now, 3 can take a quick shot if he is open, pass to either 5 or 1 for a muscle shot at the low *post*, or throw it to 4 in the corner. If none of this is possible, he can get it back outside to 2 who is in the middle of the court. *(Diagram 4-57)*

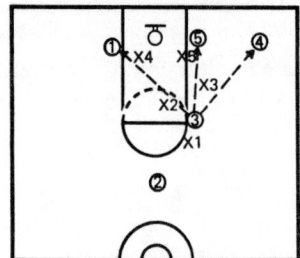

Diagram 4-57

If the ball goes to 4, he should look to *penetrate* and get the *good percentage shot* or to dump it inside to 5 at the low *post*. This places three men (1, 5, and 4) inside to work the *boards* while 3 and 2 are back to *stop the break*. 2 will balance with the ball if it is passed to 4 in the corner. *(Diagram 4-58)*

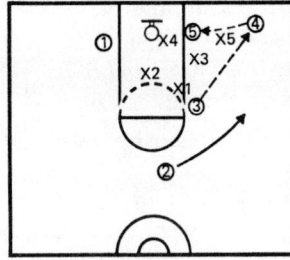

Diagram 4-58

ROTATION

If nothing goes from the original overload, the ball is passed to 2 who dribbles over to a side position out in front on the other side. 5 moves out to a forward spot and 4 drops down a few steps. 1 returns to a guard spot out front. *(Diagram 4-59)*

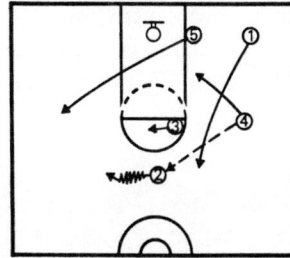

Diagram 4-59

The initial alignment has been re-established. 2 can pass to 5 and begin the same motion again or he can pass across to 1 who will hit 4 and start it on the other side. *(Diagram 4-60)*

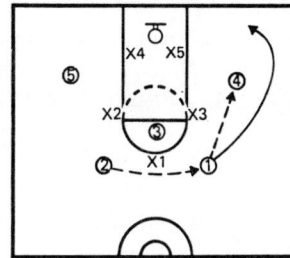

Diagram 4-60

ROTATION

If, in the original motion, 4 passed the ball from the corner to 2 on the side, 1 would come out to a guard position as 5 returned to the high post and 3 went to the forward spot on the other side. The players have now returned to their original positions and are ready to run the same motion again. *(Diagram 4-61)*

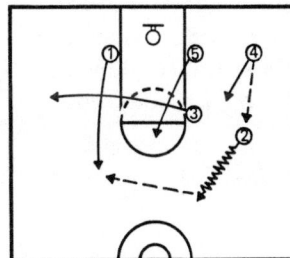

Diagram 4-61

Attack number 4

Man and Ball Movement	Outside Shooting	Tempo of Attackers	Low Post Action	Size
Considerable	Normal	Rapid	Normal	Normal

The guard with the ball tries to *split the seam* between X1 and X2. As he does so, 5 rolls to the low *post* on the ball side looking for a pass from 1. 4 keeps his eye on X5—if he crosses over the lane to cover 5, 4 should drop down low to receive a pass at the basket from 1. If not, he will come to the area of the high *post*. *(Diagram 4-62)*

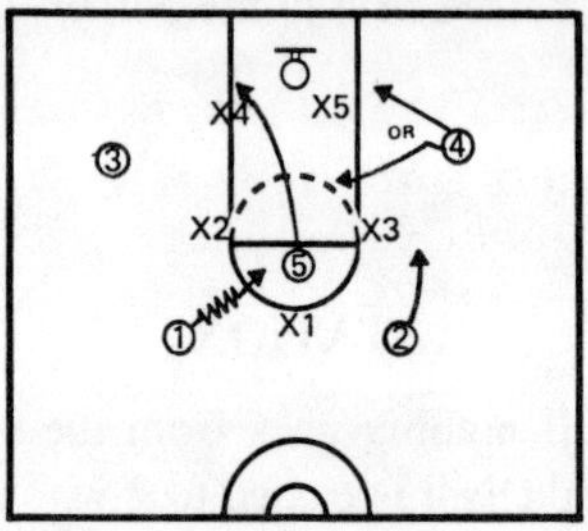

Diagram 4-62

If X4 has covered 5 at the low post, 1 should pass to 3 at the wing who may be open for the *good percentage shot from the perimeter*. 2 moves down to a spot even with 1 expecting a pass if X3 has dropped low to help cover 4 near the basket. *(Diagram 4-63)*

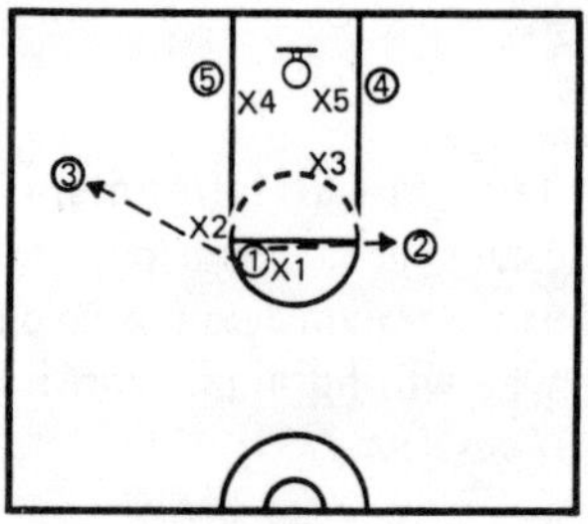

Diagram 4-63

After hitting 3, 1 continues through and out to the wing position on the other side. 2 fills the spot vacated by 1 and 4 moves out front to take 2's initial position. *(Diagram 4-64)*

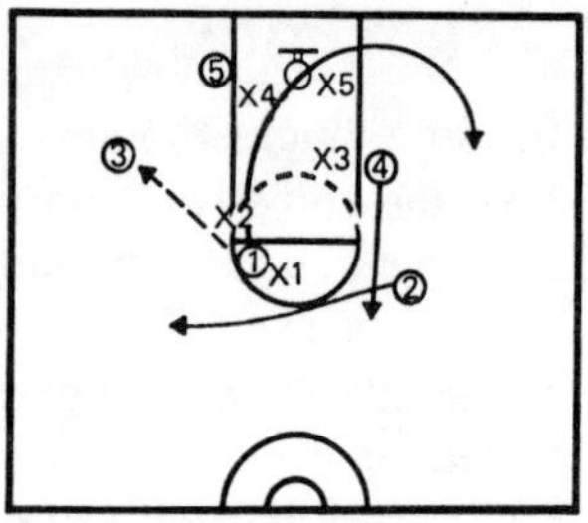

Diagram 4-64

ROTATION

Now the *ball is moved quickly* after the *movement of the men*. It goes to 2 and then to 4. 4 makes the same attempt to *split the seam* as 1 did on the other side. 5 moves across the lane to the low *post* while 3 moves either to the high or low *post* on the off-ball side in accordance with the play of the defense. *(Diagram 4-65)*

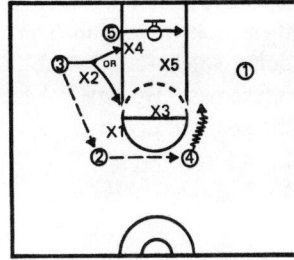

Diagram 4-65

The same action takes place again with 4 looking to pass to 3, 5, or 4 after crashing the seam. If he passes to 1, he rotates through as 1 had done on the other side. *(Diagram 4-66)*

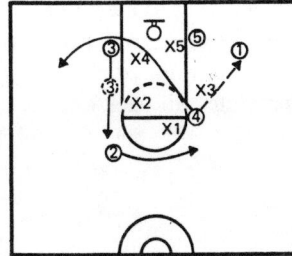

Diagram 4-66

Attack number 5

Man and Ball Movement	Outside Shooting	Tempo of Attackers	Low Post Action	Size
Considerable	Normal	Rapid	Normal	Normal

The emphasis in this style of attack is on the *rapid movement of men and ball*. A guard starts the offense by passing to the wing on his side. 5 moves down the lane and out to the corner on the ball side. Following him as a cutter down the lane is the other guard. If he does not receive a pass from 3, he moves out to the wing position on the off-ball side. 4 replaces 2 at the guard position out front. *(Diagram 4-67)*

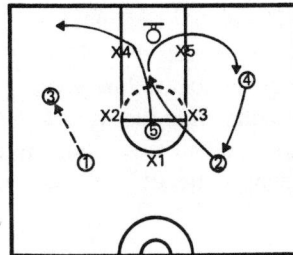

Diagram 4-67

If 3 does not hit the cutting guard, he should
then look to pass to 5 in the corner. After
doing so, he cuts to the basket expecting a
return pass. He establishes a low *post*. 1 fills
the spot vacated by 3 and 4 takes his place.
2, in turn, moves out to fill the spot vacated
by 2. *(Diagram 4-68)*

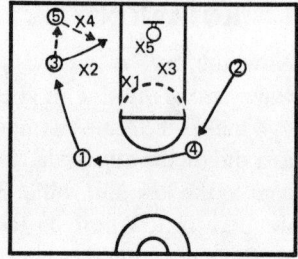

Diagram 4-68

ROTATION

If 5 cannot hit 3, he passes back out to 1 and
then moves to the corner on the other side of
the court. 3 goes from his low post to the
off-side wing position as soon as he sees 5
pass the ball back outside. 1 passes out to 4
at the guard spot. *(Diagram 4-69)*

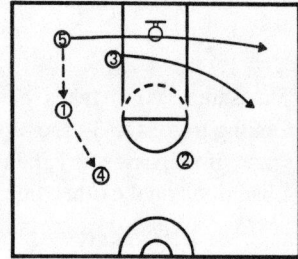

Diagram 4-69

4 passes to 2 and *cuts down the lane* looking
for a pass as soon as 2 passes to 3 at the wing
position. If he does not receive a pass, he
bends back and out to the wing spot on the
side away from the ball. *(Diagram 4-70)*

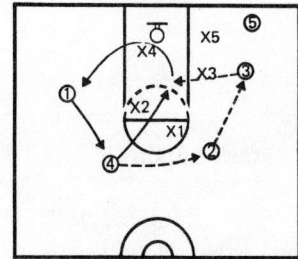

Diagram 4-70

The motion continues as before on the other
side. 3 passes to 5 in the corner and then
moves to the low *post*. 2 fills 3's spot, 1
comes from the wing to take the guard spot
on the ball side, and 4 returns to the guard
spot on the off-ball side. *(Diagram 4-71)*

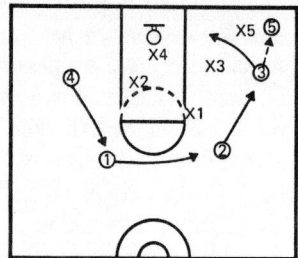

Diagram 4-71

Attack number 6

Man and Ball Movement	Outside Shooting	Tempo of Attackers	Low Post Action	Size
Limited	Normal	Normal	Stressed	Normal

The wings drop down low in this offense to match up with the two low men in the defense. 1 starts the attack with a pass to 2. 4 picks X5, and 3 comes across the lane and behind the screen looking for a pass. 5 rolls away from the side of the pass to a low *post* position, and 1 drops down to a position near the free throw line. *(Diagram 4-72)*

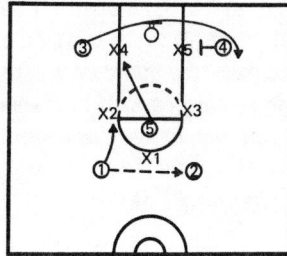

Diagram 4-72

2 now attempts to *penetrate* the defense by *splitting the seam* between X1 and X3. The intention is to draw the two men to him. If he is successful, one of his teammates should be open for a pass and a *good percentage shot*. He may pass directly inside to 3, 4, or 5. X4 and X5 may be able to adjust to the play of 3 and 4, but this puts great pressure on X2. 2 should watch his action carefully. If he does not drop back quickly, a lob pass to 5 at the basket will result in an easy shot. If X2 does cover, 1 should be wide open for the pass and a *good percentage shot*. *(Diagram 4-73)*

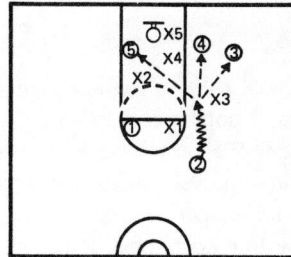

Diagram 4-73

If 1 receives a pass, 5 may either step out to the side quickly or *pick* X2 if he is close, so that 4 can come across the lane and receive a pass behind the screen for a *good percentage shot*. The same circumstances now exist on the other side and 1 should be aware of the new possibilities. *(Diagram 4-74)*

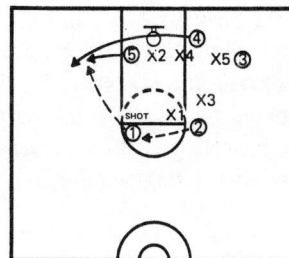

Diagram 4-74

Attack number 7

Man and Ball Movement	Outside Shooting	Tempo of Attackers	Low Post Action	Size
Normal	Normal	Slow	Stressed	Normal

The attack begins with a pass from a guard out front (2) to the wing on his side (4). After the pass, the guard cuts to the basket looking for a return pass. If he does not receive it, he bends out to the corner on the ball side. 3 drops down low on the off-ball side. *(Diagram 4-75)*

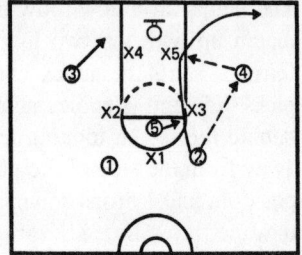

Diagram 4-75

5 now rolls to the low *post* on the ball side and 3 pops across to a mid-*post* on the same side. We now have an *overloaded* situation and 4 may shoot from his position in the *gap* if he is open or pass to 2 in the corner, 5 at the low *post*, or 3 at the mid-*post*. 1 drops down to a point near the free-throw line extended on the off-ball side. *(Diagram 4-76)*

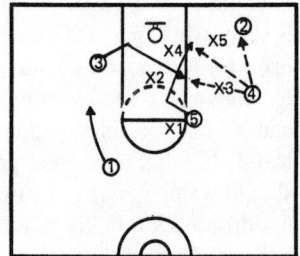

Diagram 4-76

If the pass goes to 2 in the corner, 4 moves out to the guard position on the ball side. If 2 does not have a shot, he dribbles outside looking to pass to 3 at the high *post*. After the pass, 2 goes to set a *screen* for 5 at the low post. *(Diagram 4-77)*

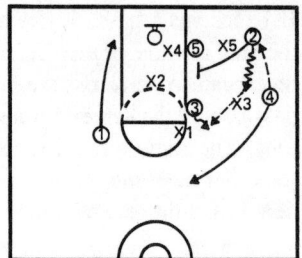

Diagram 4-77

From this position 3 may pass to 5 stepping out from behind the screen for the *good percentage shot* or he may pass back out front to 4. *(Diagram 4-78)*

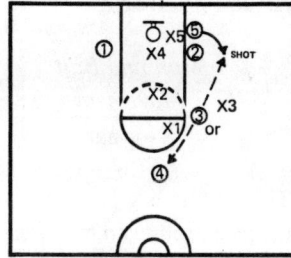

Diagram 4-78

ROTATION

1 pops out to the wing and receives a pass from 4 who then cuts down the lane and out to the corner if he does not receive a pass. 5 now flashes to the high *post* on the ball side. 3 moves down the lane to be in position to cut across the lane after the roll to the basket by 5. 2 comes outside to the free-throw line extended. *(Diagram 4-79)*

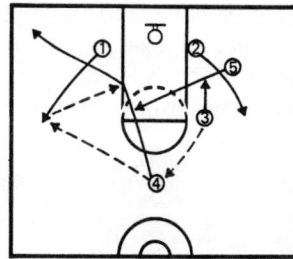

Diagram 4-79

The same action now takes place on this side as was described on the other side. *(Diagram 4-80)*

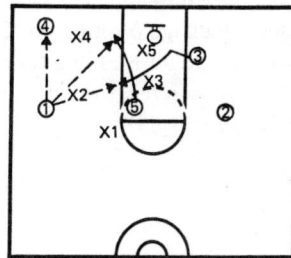

Diagram 4-80

Once again, if the ball goes into the corner, it will be brought out in the same manner as before and rotated to the other side. *(Diagram 4-81)*

Diagram 4-81

Attack number 8

Man and Ball Movement	Outside Shooting	Tempo of Attackers	Low Post Action	Size
Normal	Normal	Rapid	Stressed	Normal

The motion begins with a guard (1) to guard (2) pass, followed by a flash to the open spot in the middle by 4. If possible, 2 should get him the ball because he would have a good opportunity for a jump shot in a *good percentage shooting area*. 3 drops to the low *post* looking for a pass from 4 if X4 comes up to cover 4. 5 steps out to the corner from his low post position. *(Diagram 4-82)*

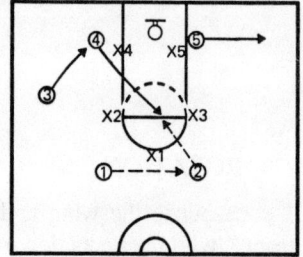

Diagram 4-82

If 2 can't pass the ball to 4, he moves it to 5 in the corner. As this happens, 4 rolls to the low *post* looking for a pass from 5 if he can get advantage position on X4. 2 quickly goes to the high *post* hoping for a pass and a shot. 1 moves over to fill 2's vacated spot. *(Diagram 4-83)*

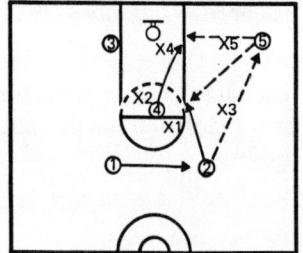

Diagram 4-83

ROTATION

If 5 cannot hit either man, he passes back out to 1 at a guard spot. 3 comes out to the guard spot from his weakside low post as 4 fills his position and 5 moves into the low *post* from his position in the corner. The ball is passed from 1 to 3. *(Diagram 4-84)*

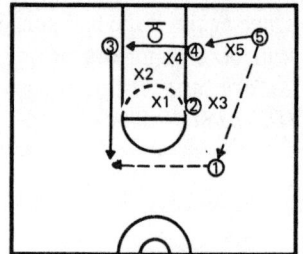

Diagram 4-84

Now 5 flashes to the open spot in the 1-2-2 zone. 4 steps to the corner and 2 moves out to a wing. *(Diagram 4-85)*

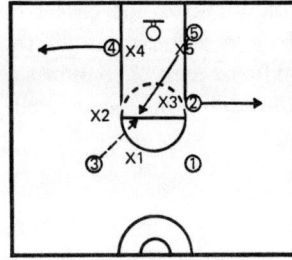

Diagram 4-85

If 3 can't get the ball to 5 in the middle, he passes to 4 in the corner. When that happens, 5 rolls to the basket hoping to get advantage position on X5 and 1 dives to the open spot in the middle of the zone. *(Diagram 4-86)*

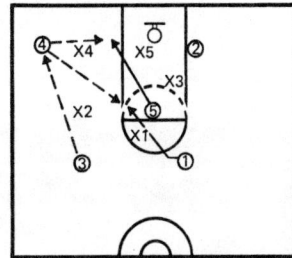

Diagram 4-86

ATTACKING A 1-2-2 ZONE FROM A 2-2-1 ALIGNMENT

Attack number 1

Man and Ball Movement	Outside Shooting	Tempo of Attackers	Low Post Action	Size
Considerable	Normal	Rapid	Normal	Normal

2 passes to 4 and cuts to the basket hoping for a return pass. 1 fills 2's vacated spot. 3 angles out and around the circle to be prepared to follow 2's cut. 5 moves up from his low *post* on the off-ball side. *(Diagram 4-87)*

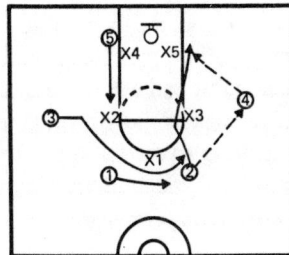

Diagram 4-87

3 now cuts to the basket hoping for a pass from 4 somewhere in the *gap* near the mid-*post* area. 2 continues across the lane to a low *post* on the off-ball side. *(Diagram 4-88)*

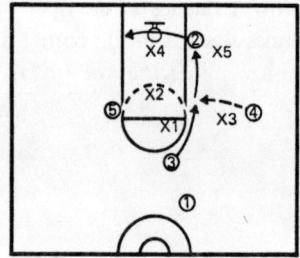

Diagram 4-88

5 now becomes the third cutter in the same manner as with 2 and 3. *(Diagram 4-89)*

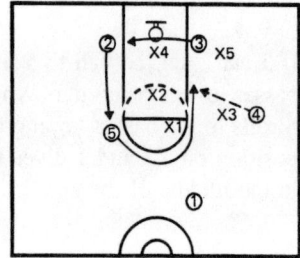

Diagram 4-89

ROTATION

4 backs the ball out to 1 who then swings it to 2 near the high *post*. 3 steps out halfway into the corner to receive a pass from 2, and 5 comes across to the low *post* hopefully in front of X5. *(Diagram 4-90)*

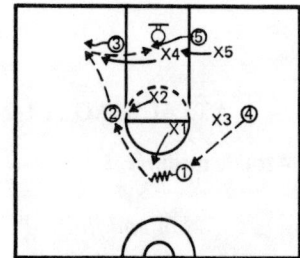

Diagram 4-90

Option. In the beginning of the motion, 2 may go into the corner rather than across the lane. The ball can be passed to him there and if he does not have a shot, he can look to feed 3 cutting to the basket or to 5 coming to the *gap* near the mid-*post* area. 1 fills 2's vacated spot. *(Diagram 4-91)*

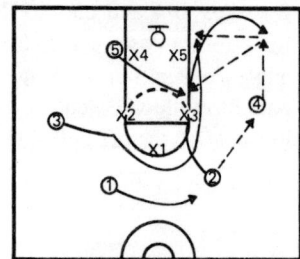

Diagram 4-91

ROTATION

2 passes back to 4 and he in turn passes out to 1 in front. 3 continues across and out to a spot near the high post on the off-ball side and 5 moves halfway out to the corner. 2 goes to a low *post* on the off-ball side. *(Diagram 4-92)*

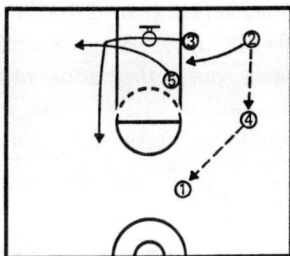

Diagram 4-92

5 looks for the *good percentage shot* or to dump the ball into 2 at a spot near the basket for a muscle shot. *(Diagram 4-93)*

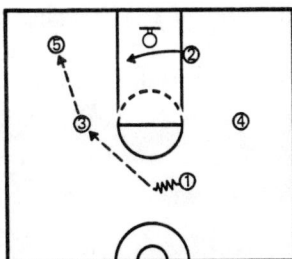

Diagram 4-93

Attack number 2

Man and Ball Movement	Outside Shooting	Tempo of Attackers	Low Post Action	Size
Considerable	Necessary	Slow	Normal	Normal

The strong side guard begins the motion by passing to the wing (3). The weak side guard (2) cuts into the heart of the zone where it is open looking for a pass and a quick jump shot. If he does not receive the pass, he continues down the lane and out to the weak side. 5 moves to the corner and 4 fills the cutting guard's vacated spot. *(Diagram 4-94)*

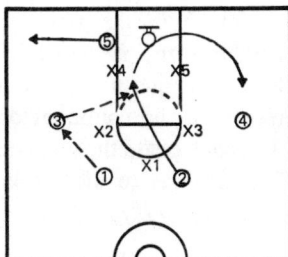

Diagram 4-94

3 now passes to 5 in the corner and then
flashes to the low *post* while 2 comes to an
open spot in the middle of the zone looking
for a quick pass and a jump shot. 1 fills the
wing and 4 takes the point. *(Diagram 4-95)*

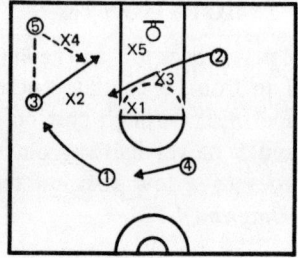

Diagram 4-95

ROTATION

5 passes to 1 at the wing position and then
moves across the lane to a low post. 3 continues across the lane and out to a wing position. *(Diagram 4-96)*

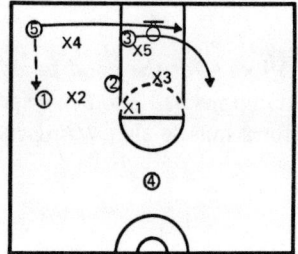

Diagram 4-96

The ball is moved to the point (4) and then to
the wing (3) as 5 steps out to the corner.
(Diagram 4-97)

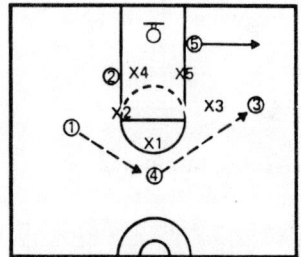

Diagram 4-97

As 3 receives the pass, 1 is cutting into the
middle of the open area in the zone looking
for a pass and a quick shot. If he does not
receive it, he continues down the lane and
then back out to the wing on the off-ball side.
2 moves out to the weak side guard spot.
(Diagram 4-98)

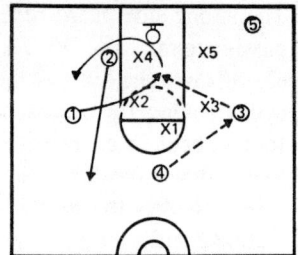

Diagram 4-98

3 now passes to 5 in the corner, goes to the low post as 1 flashes to an open spot in the middle of the zone. 4 fills 3's vacated wing position. *(Diagram 4-99)*

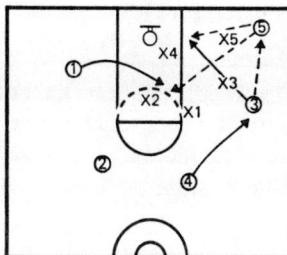

Diagram 4-99

ATTACKING A 1-2-2 ZONE FROM A 2-3 ALIGNMENT

Attack number 1

Man and Ball Movement	Outside Shooting	Tempo of Attackers	Low Post Action	Size
Normal	Normal	Slow	Stressed	Big men

In this alignment we start with a stack on one side and a single low post on the other. The bottom man in the tandem post steps out behind 4's *screen* looking for a pass from 2 and a quick jump shot in the *good percentage shooting area*. He may also dump the ball inside to 4 at the low *post* if he is in an advantage position. As this is happening, 1 moves into the middle and 3 positions himself on the off-side looking for the rebound. *(Diagram 4-100)*

Diagram 4-100

1 continues down the lane, goes under 4's low post and out to an open spot near the baseline looking for a pass from 5. In the meantime, 5 has started a dribble out toward the wing position. The *overload* has now been accomplished. *(Diagram 4-101)*

Diagram 4-101

ROTATION

To rotate, 5 passes out to 2 and cuts through to a wing position on the other side. 4 comes across the lane to a low *post* on the ball side. 3 comes out to a guard spot to receive a pass from 2. After the pass, 2 cuts through under 4's post to an open spot near the baseline. 1 comes out to the point position. *(Diagram 4-102)*

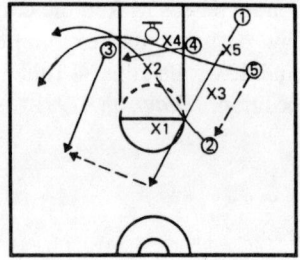

Diagram 4-102

The same opportunities now exist on the other side and the rotation remains the same. *(Diagram 4-103)*

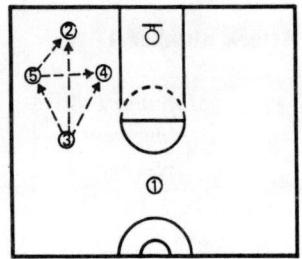

Diagram 4-103

Attack number 2

Man and Ball Movement	Outside Shooting	Tempo of Attackers	Low Post Action	Size
Considerable	Necessary	Rapid	Normal	Normal

A guard (1) passes to a wing (3) and cuts through to the opposite corner. 2 steps over to fill 1's vacated spot. *(Diagram 4-104)*

Diagram 4-104

3 passes to 2 at the point. 2 then passes to 5 at the wing on the strong side. As this happens, 4 rolls to the low *post* and 3 flashes to a high *post* in the middle of the zone. 5 may pass to either 3, 4, or 1 in the corner in this *overload* situation. 1 in turn may shoot if he is open or pass to either 4 or 3 if they have an advantage position. *(Diagram 4-105)*

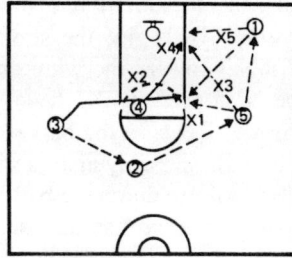

Diagram 4-105

ROTATION

If none of this goes, the ball is swung out to 5 and then to 3 who steps out to a guard spot from his high post. 1 goes to the other corner, 4 comes out to the wing, and 2 rotates over to the other guard spot. *(Diagram 4-106)*

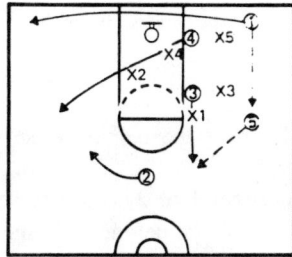

Diagram 4-106

Now the ball is passed from 3 to 2, followed by a cut to the low *post* on the strong side by 3 and a flash to the high *post* by 5. 2 passes quickly to 4 who will then have the same *overloaded* possibilities as were available on the other side. The rotation remains the same. *(Diagram 4-107)*

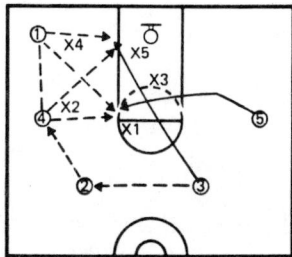

Diagram 4-107

Attack number 3

Man and Ball Movement	Outside Shooting	Tempo of Attackers	Low Post Action	Size
Considerable	Necessary	Rapid	Normal	Normal

In this alignment one man is set in the corner. To begin, the strongside guard (2) dribbles toward the wing on his side. After he is stopped by X3 he passes to 5 in the corner. 2 cuts to the basket hoping for a return pass and a lay up or a short jump shot. 5 also looks to dump the ball inside to 4 at the low *post* if he has advantage position. Of course 5 may take the shot from the corner if X5 does not move out to take him quickly. 1 rotates over to fill 2's spot. *(Diagram 4-108)*

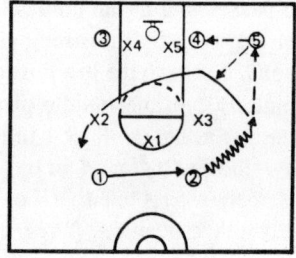

Diagram 4-108

If 5 gets the ball to 4, several things may happen: first, he may shoot, he may pass out to either 1 or 2 who may be sitting in open spots as the defense adjusts, or he may pass across to 3 at the low *post* if X2 has not dropped back to cover. *(Diagram 4-109)*

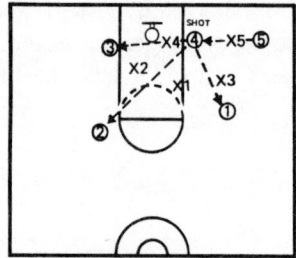

Diagram 4-109

ROTATION

If 5 can't pass to 4, he swings the ball out to 1. This keys 3's break to the high post in an attempt to receive a pass from 1. After the pass the guards run a double cut off the post, 1 going through and to the other guard spot, and 2 going by and then out to a wing. Either may receive a handoff for a *drive* to the basket or a quick jump shot in the *good percentage shooting area*. 4 goes to the low post on the other side and 5 crosses to the other corner. *(Diagram 4-110)*

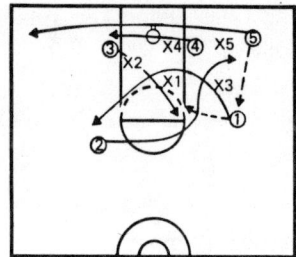

Diagram 4-110

If 3 can't get a shot or give the ball to either guard, he passes out front to the first cutting guard (1) and then drops down to the low post on the weak side. Now 1 passes to 5 in the corner and the motion begins again. *(Diagram 4-111)*

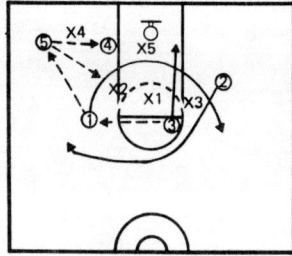

Diagram 4-111

ROTATION

If 1 can't hit 3 at the high post, he can bypass him, moving the ball to 2. From here, the motion remains the same. *(Diagram 4-112)*

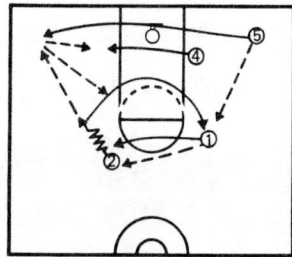

Diagram 4-112

Chapter 5

HOW TO ATTACK THE 1-3-1 ZONE DEFENSE

ATTACKING A 1-3-1 FROM A 1-2-2 ALIGNMENT

Attack number 1

Man and Ball Movement	Outside Shooting	Tempo of Attackers	Low Post Action	Size
Normal	Necessary	Rapid	Unstressed	Not major factor

The 1-2-2 alignment is set to the side. 2 is in the corner and 3 is near the sideline. 1 brings the ball up about a step to the side of the lane on the strong side. He passes to 3. 3 then passes to the corner and cuts to the basket expecting a return pass. If 2 is not covered in the corner he may shoot. 1 fills 3's vacated spot. *(Diagram 5-1)*

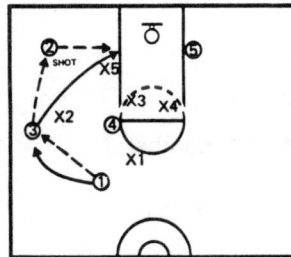

Diagram 5-1

ROTATION

2 passes outside to 1 at the wing. 4 moves
out to the point position and receives a pass
from 1 as 2 crosses into the other corner and
5 moves out to a wing spot on the side away
from the ball. *(Diagram 5-2)*

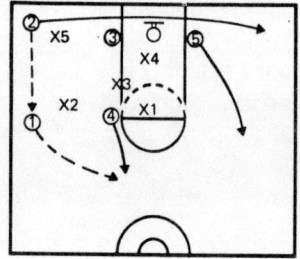

Diagram 5-2

4 now swings the ball to 5 who may shoot if
he is not covered. 3 comes to the strong side
high *post* and 1 goes directly to the basket. If
1 is not covered 5 may lob him the ball behind the defensive men coming to the ball
side. *(Diagram 5-3)*

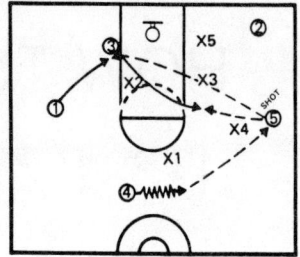

Diagram 5-3

If 1 or 3 is not open, 5 should pass the ball to
2 in the corner and cut to the basket expecting a return pass. If 2 is not covered in the
corner, he may shoot. 4 fills 5's vacated
spot. The motion continues as before.
(Diagram 5-4)

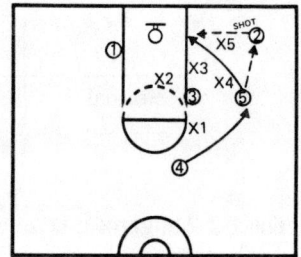

Diagram 5-4

Attack number 2

Man and Ball Movement	Outside Shooting	Tempo of Attackers	Low Post Action	Size
Normal	Normal	Rapid	Stressed	Normal

This motion emphasizes quick *movement* of both ball and players. 1 starts by passing to a wing (3) and cutting through to the baseline on the side away from the pass. 5 *screens* X5 and 4 comes under it looking for a pass from 3 and a shot in a *good percentage shooting area*. 2 fills 1's vacated spot. *(Diagram 5-5)*

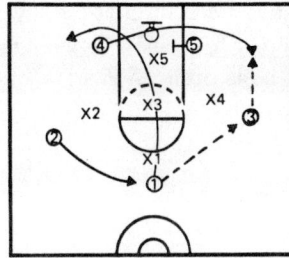

Diagram 5-5

From the triangle, either 3 or 4 can hit 5 at the low *post* if he has advantage position on X3. *(Diagram 5-6)*

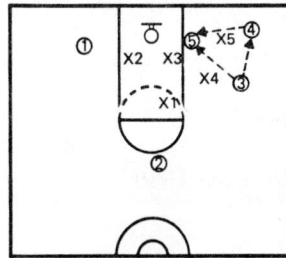

Diagram 5-6

After 3 passes to 4, he cuts through to the wing on the other side. 1 and 2 rotate over to cover vacated spots. *(Diagram 5-7)*

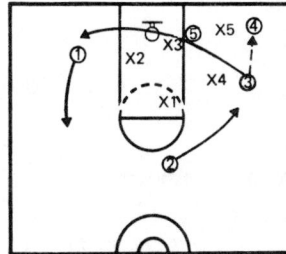

Diagram 5-7

ROTATION

The ball is now passed back out to 2. 2 swings the ball to 1 and dives through to the corner on the other side. 1 passes to 3 and cuts down the lane to a position for the off-side *rebound*. 4 rolls across the lane to the low *post* looking for advantage position. *(Diagram 5-8)*

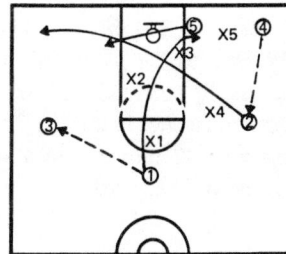

Diagram 5-8

Now 3 can hit 5 at the low *post* or 2 in the corner for a shot. 2 can dump the ball into 5 if he is open. *(5-9)*

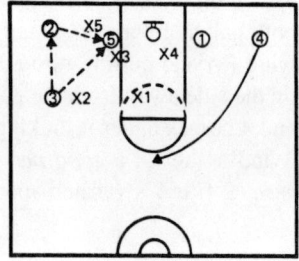

Diagram 5-9

After 3's pass he cuts through to the other side, 4 fills down, and 1 steps out to a wing. *(Diagram 5-10)*

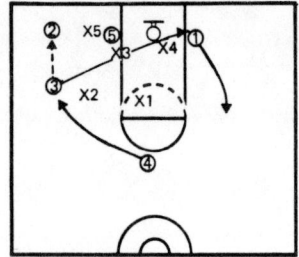

Diagram 5-10

Attack number 3

Man and Ball Movement	Outside Shooting	Tempo of Attackers	Low Post Action	Size
Limited	Necessary	Slow	Stressed	Normal

1 passes to 3 at the wing and then cuts down the lane to the weak side low post. 4 goes across the lane under 5's *screen* looking for a pass and a shot in the *good percentage shooting area*. 2 moves into a side-post position on the off-ball side. *(Diagram 5-11)*

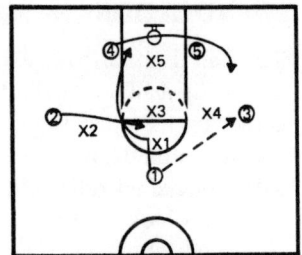

Diagram 5-11

3 now attempts to *penetrate* the *gap* between X1 and X4. This places the stress of covering four offensive men in a *good percentage shooting area* by only three defensive men. 3 needs to be alert to the defensive reaction to know who is open. If X5 does not fight around the *screen*, 4 will have a shot. If X3 does not front 5 he may have advantage position at the low *post*. If X2 does not drop back, 1 may have a shot at the basket. If X2 does drop back, 2 should be open for a short jumper. *(Diagram 5-12)*

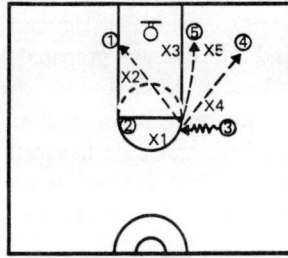

Diagram 5-12

If 3 passes to 2, 5 comes across the lane under 1's *screen* as 3 moves down to weakside low *post*. 4 steps up to a side-post on the off-ball side. *(Diagram 5-13)*

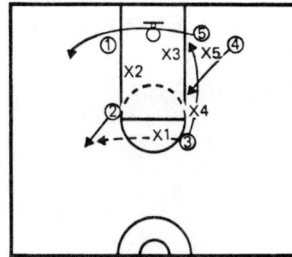

Diagram 5-13

Now the same offensive opportunities exist again as 2 attempts to *penetrate* the *gap* between X2 and X1. *(Diagram 5-14)*

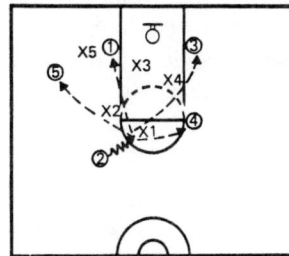

Diagram 5-14

ATTACKING A 1-3-1 ZONE FROM A 1-3-1 ALIGNMENT

Attack number 1

Man and Ball Movement	Outside Shooting	Tempo of Attackers	Low Post Action	Size
Considerable	Necessary	Rapid	Stressed	Normal

Point man 1 begins by passing to the wing on the strongside (3). He then goes around him and into the lane prepared to set a screen on X3 as he drops low to cover. 4 goes to the corner on the ball side. 5 rolls low away from the ball, and 2 flashes to the high *post* from the off-ball side-wing position. *(Diagram 5-15)*

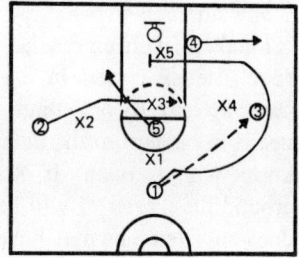

Diagram 5-15

3 passes the ball to 4 in the corner. 4 may now hit 5 coming across the lane behind 1's *screen* or pass to 2 at the high *post*. He may also have a shot from the corner if X5 does not come out to challenge him immediately. *(Diagram 5-16)*

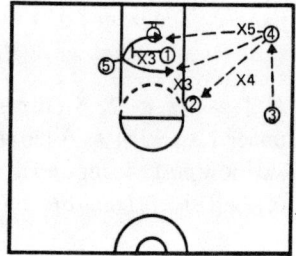

Diagram 5-16

ROTATION

4 backs the ball out to 3 and returns to the low post. 3 dribbles out to the point as 5 returns to the high *post*. 1 and 2 go to the wing positions in the 1-3-1 alignment. *(Diagram 5-17)*

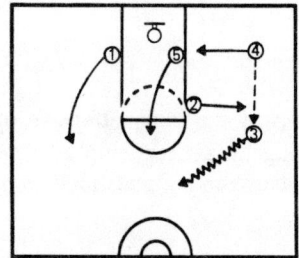

Diagram 5-17

Now 3 passes to 1 and goes around him into the strongside corner. 4 comes to the strongside high *post* as 5 drops down to the low *post* near the basket. 2 now fills the point position. *(Diagram 5-18)*

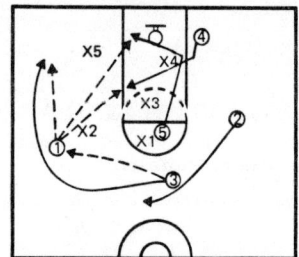

Diagram 5-18

If 1 hits 3 in the corner, he should look to dump the ball inside to 5 near the basket or out to 4 at the high *post*. *(Diagram 5-19)*

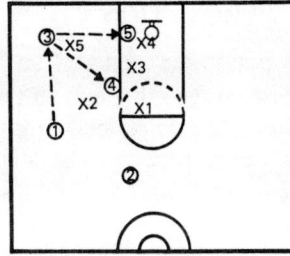

Diagram 5-19

If nothing is open the ball is passed back out to 1. He dribbles to the point as 2 and 3 take the wing spots. 5 returns to the high *post* and 4 goes back to his original low *post* set. It's obvious that from the initial alignment there is a weak side and a strong side. To start the motion, the ball may be passed to either side. The appropriate action is then taken by all players as illustrated in the diagram. *(Diagram 5-20)*

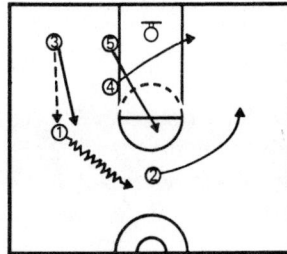

Diagram 5-20

Attack number 2

Man and Ball Movement	Outside Shooting	Tempo of Attackers	Low Post Action	Size
Normal	Necessary	Rapid	Normal	Normal

This is a very simple but effective motion that emphasizes *quick movement*. The point man (1) passes to the wing (3) on the strong side. This is followed by 3's pass to 4 who has moved into the corner. 3 cuts to the basket hoping to get a return pass near the basket. 5 rolls to the basket hoping for the same thing. 1 fills 3's vacated spot and 2 fills 1's original spot. *(Diagram 5-21)*

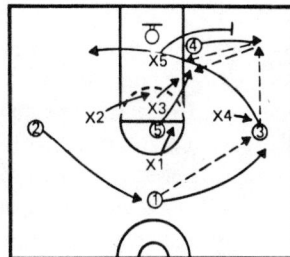

Diagram 5-21

ROTATION

4 passes back out to 1 and goes to the low *post* on the other side. 5 returns to the high *post* and 3 comes out to the wing on his side. 1 passes to 2 and the alignment is re-set. *(Diagram 5-22)*

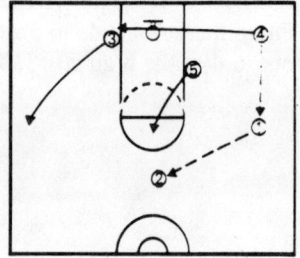

Diagram 5-22

The same thing occurs again on this side. 2 passes to 3 who in turn passes to 4 in the corner followed by 3's cut to the basket and 5's roll to the basket. 2 and 1 fill the vacated spots. *(Diagram 5-23)*

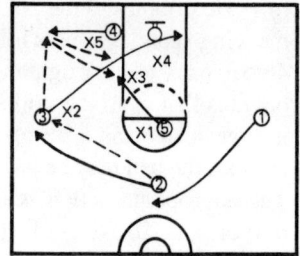

Diagram 5-23

Attack number 3

Man and Ball Movement	Outside Shooting	Tempo of Attackers	Low Post Action	Size
Limited	Normal	Normal	Stressed	Normal

The point man (1) begins by dribbling to a side and forcing the defensive wing on that side (X4) to come up. If X5 leaves to cover the wing (3) who drops down to a spot near the baseline, 1 can fire the ball directly to 4 at the basket. If X5 does not move out, 1 can pass to 3 for a quick shot or a pass inside to 4. 2 steps outside to take the guard spot. *(Diagram 5-24)*

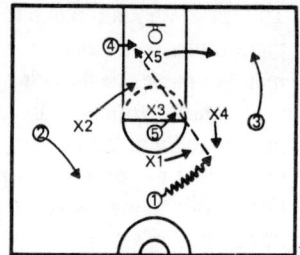

Diagram 5-24

If nothing is open, the ball is swung to the other side. 1 passes to 2 and 2 duplicates the action of 1 on the other side looking for the same opportunities as before. *(Diagram 5-25)*

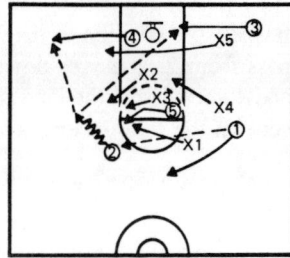

Diagram 5-25

Attack number 4

Man and Ball Movement	Outside Shooting	Tempo of Attackers	Low Post Action	Size
Considerable	Necessary	Rapid	Unstressed	Normal

1 passes to the wing on the strong side (3). The ball is then moved to 5 in the corner. After this pass 3 flashes to the low *post* looking for a return pass as 4 attempts to gain an advantage position over X3 at a mid-post position. 1 fills 3's wing position and 2 moves to the point. *(Diagram 5-26)*

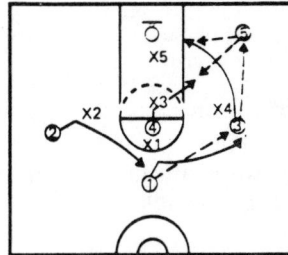

Diagram 5-26

5 will have a shot if X5 does not move out on him quickly. If he cannot hit 3 or 4 with a pass, he backs the ball out to 1 at a wing position. 3 continues across to the low post on the off-ball side and 4 moves down to the baseline. *(Diagram 5-27)*

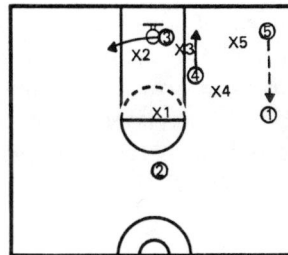

Diagram 5-27

As 1 passes the ball out to 2 at the point, 5 flashes to a position in the *gap* looking for a pass from 2. 1 moves down into the corner and 4 goes across the lane and out to an open spot on the side under 3's screen. *(Diagram 5-28)*

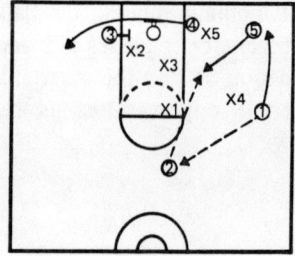

Diagram 5-28

If 2 is able to hit 5 near the middle, 5 may have an opportunity for a quick jump shot from the *good percentage shooting area*, or he may be able to pass to either 1, 3, or 4 in an open area depending on the reaction of the defense. *(Diagram 5-29)*

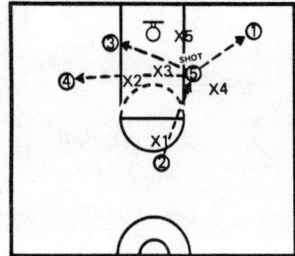

Diagram 5-29

If 2 cannot pass to 5, 3, should flash to the high *post* looking for a pass while 5 drops down to fill his vacated low *post* position. *(Diagram 5-30)*

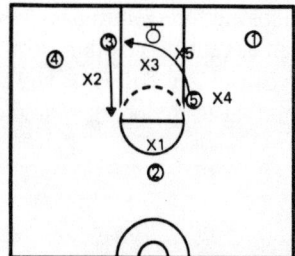

Diagram 5-30

If the ball is passed to 3, a quick jump shot is possible again from the *good percentage shooting area*, and again three passes are possible to players in position to score: to 1 and 5 at the baseline and 4 at the wing. *(Diagram 5-31)*

Diagram 5-31

Attack number 5

Man and Ball Movement	Outside Shooting	Tempo of Attackers	Low Post Action	Size
Considerable	Normal	Rapid	Stressed	Normal

1 passes to a wing (4) and 3 rolls to the strong side baseline as 5 comes to the open spot in the middle over or under X3 (depending on where he is playing). *(Diagram 5-32)*

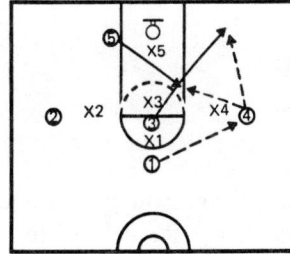

Diagram 5-32

If neither man is open, 4 passes back out to 1 at the point and runs through to the baseline on the other side of the lane. 1 swings the ball to 2 at the other wing. *(Diagram 5-33)*

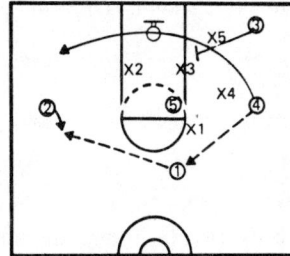

Diagram 5-33

Now 2 hits 4 and cuts to the basket looking for a return pass. 3 comes across from the other side to a low *post* on the strong side hoping for advantage position. This action should keep the deep defensive man busy from corner to corner. 1 moves over to fill 2's vacated spot. *(Diagram 5-34)*

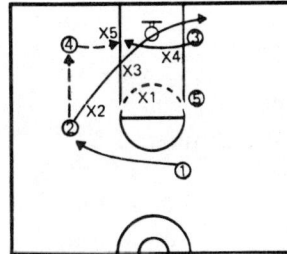

Diagram 5-34

Now 4 passes out to 1 and goes to the opposite corner. 2 comes out from the weakside baseline to receive a pass from 1 at the guard spot. *(Diagram 5-35)*

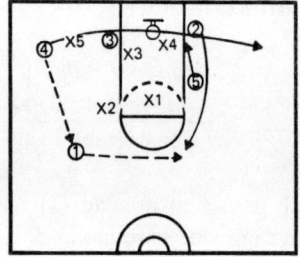

Diagram 5-35

2 quickly swings the ball to 4 who may have a shot if the defense has not been able to adjust. 2 cuts through looking for a return pass and 3 comes off his cut to the open spot hoping for a pass and a shot. 5 is attempting to get advantage position at the low *post* so that he may get a pass from 4. 1 moves over to fill 2's spot. *(Diagram 5-36)*

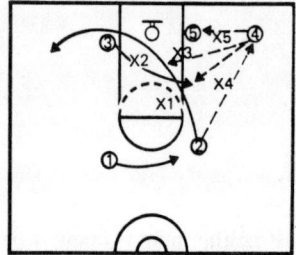

Diagram 5-36

If 4 cannot hit any of these men he passes back out to 1 and the rotation continues. *(Diagram 5-37)*

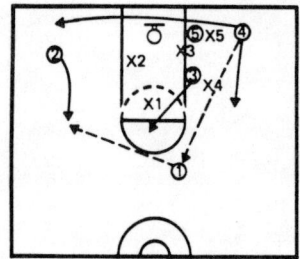

Diagram 5-37

Attack number 6

Man and Ball Movement	Outside Shooting	Tempo of Attackers	Low Post Action	Size
Normal	Necessary	Rapid	Stressed	Normal

Simplicity and quickness of ball and man movement make this an effective offense against the 1-3-1 zone. The point man passes to the wing on the strong side (3). 4 steps in to *screen* the deep defensive man as 5 comes under the screen looking for a pass and a jump shot. 5 may dump the ball into 4 at the low *post* if he has advantage position. *(Diagram 5-38)*

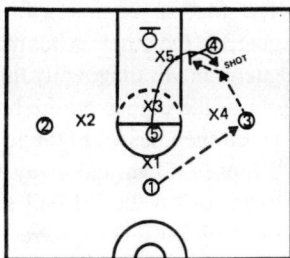

Diagram 5-38

ROTATION

To rotate, 3 passes back out to 1. 1 swings the ball to 2 at the other wing. 4 steps across the lane to a low *post* and 3 quickly flashes under the *screen* looking for a pass and a jump shot. 2 can also make a direct pass to 4 at the low post or to 5 on the other side who is in rebounding position if X4 has not gotten back quickly enough to cover him. *(Diagram 5-39)*

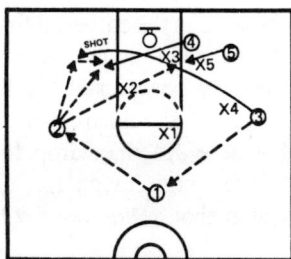

Diagram 5-39

Again, the ball is swung to the other side and the rotation remains the same. *(Diagram 5-40)*

Diagram 5-40

ATTACKING A 1-3-1 ZONE FROM A 2-1-2 ALIGNMENT

Attack number 1

Man and Ball Movement	Outside Shooting	Tempo of Attackers	Low Post Action	Size
Considerable	Necessary	Rapid	Normal	Normal

The motion begins with a pass from one guard to the other. After making the pass, the guard moves diagonally through the lane and out to the corner on the ball side. The other guard then passes to the forward on his side. 5 moves down and away from the ball to a low *post* on the off-ball side as 4 comes to the high post. *(Diagram 5-41)*

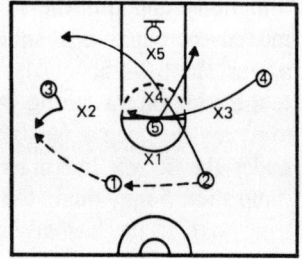

Diagram 5-41

This forces X2 to come to the ball, X5 to honor 2 in the corner. 3 first looks for 5 at the basket for a lob pass. If he gets a step on X3 he may be open at the basket for an easy lay-up. 3 should also watch 4 at the high *post* because X4 may drop low and leave him alone long enough for a quick pass and a jump shot. *(Diagram 5-42)*

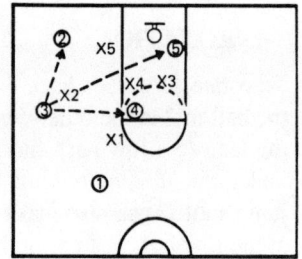

Diagram 5-42

If the ball goes to 2 in the corner, 5 should move across the lane quickly to establish a position at the low *post*. He should have a step on everyone else and may be able to receive a pass at the basket for a muscle shot. *(Diagram 5-43)*

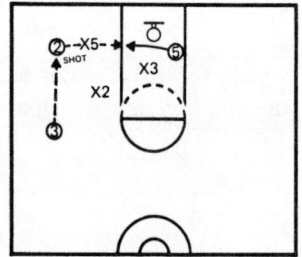

Diagram 5-43

ROTATION

If none of this is available, 3 returns the ball to 1. 1 dribbles once or twice to open up a pass to 5 who has moved out to the wing. 2 moves across the court and into the corner on the other side. 4 drops down to the low *post* on the off-ball side as 3 comes to the strong-side high *post*. *(Diagram 5-44)*

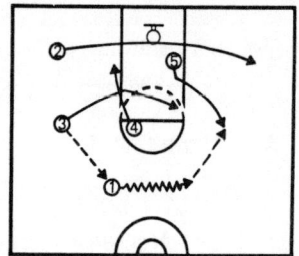

Diagram 5-44

The same opportunities as before are now available on the other side. *Quickness in the movement of the ball and men* is very important in this offense. *(Diagram 5-45)*

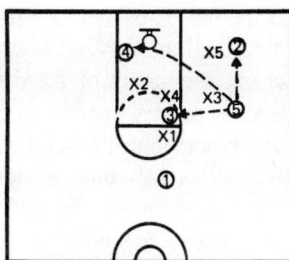

Diagram 5-45

Attack number 2

Man and Ball Movement	Outside Shooting	Tempo of Attackers	Low Post Action	Size
Normal	Normal	Rapid	Stressed	Normal

To begin, the wings are dropped down low near the baseline in this 2-1-2 set. After a pass from the other guard, 1 dribbles right at X2 to force him to commit himself to the ball. 3 steps out to the corner to put pressure on X5 to cover him. 4 moves in toward the basket slightly looking for a pass and 5 rolls to a *post* position on the ball side. *(Diagram 5-46)*

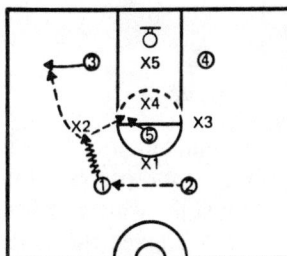

Diagram 5-46

If 1 can hit 5 at the high *post*, 4 steps back out and toward the corner and 2 drops down to a position near the free-throw line extended. This puts great pressure on X3 to cover both men. If 5 hits 2, X3 is forced out on him, giving 2 the opportunity to *move the ball quickly* to 4 who may have a *good percentage shot* from the short corner. *(Diagram 5-47)*

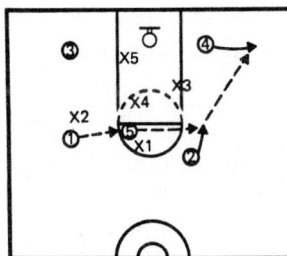

Diagram 5-47

If the ball is passed to 3 in the corner, X5 is forced all the way out to cover him. 4 should check the action of the defense (X3 in particular) and try to come to the ball at an angle of advantage to be free for a pass at the basket and a low *post* muscle shot. 5 moves down and toward the ball slightly. He may be open momentarily as X4 drops down to try to help against 4 at the basket. *(Diagram 5-48)*

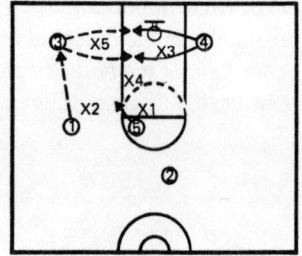

Diagram 5-48

If the ball is passed to 4, 5 should cut to the basket looking for a pass from 4. This may be possible because X3 and X4 have committed themselves to the ball and are not in position to cover 5. *(Diagram 5-49)*

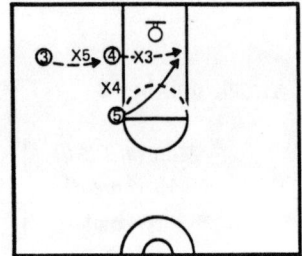

Diagram 5-49

ROTATION

If 3 cannot hit 4 or 5, he returns the ball to 1 who, in turn, passes out to 2. 2 then dribbles down at the wing as 1 had done on the other side. 4 crosses the lane and out into the corner on the ball side. 3 moves to a low *post* on the off-ball side. 5 holds until 2 is stopped by X3 at the wing. *(Diagram 5-50)*

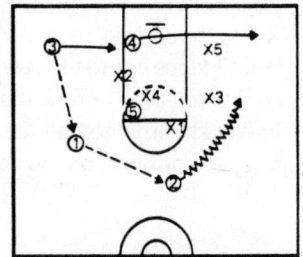

Diagram 5-50

Now the same opportunities as before are available on this side. *(Diagram 5-51)*

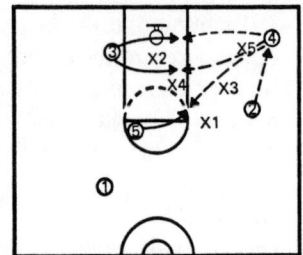

Diagram 5-51

Attack number 3

Man and Ball Movement	Outside Shooting	Tempo of Attackers	Low Post Action	Size
Normal	Necessary	Rapid	Normal	Normal

One of the guards (2) attempts to *penetrate* the *gap* between the defensive point and the wing. As he does so, 5 rolls to a low *post* on the ball side. The other guard *penetrates* with him looking for a flip pass. As the defensive wing on his side steps out to cover him, 1 passes to 3 at the wing position. *(Diagram 5-52)*

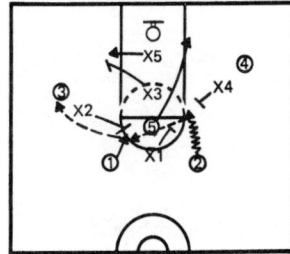

Diagram 5-52

After the pass 1 cuts through to the basket and under 5's *screen*. 3 now passes the ball outside to 2 and then the ball is swung to 4 who has opened himself up for a pass. 4 now looks to hit 1 behind 5's *screen* for the quick jump shot in the *good percentage shooting area*. *(Diagram 5-53)*

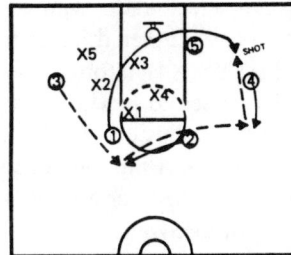

Diagram 5-53

ROTATION

After 4's pass to 1 he cuts through and out to the other side. 5 goes back to his original high post and 3 and 2 move over to be in position to swing the ball. *(Diagram 5-54)*

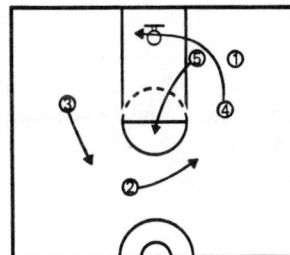

Diagram 5-54

The ball is now quickly swung from 1 to 2 and then to 3. 5 rolls low providing a *screen* for 4 to shoot behind. *(Diagram 5-55)*

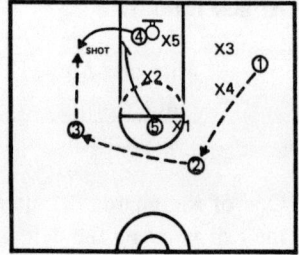

Diagram 5-55

Attack number 4

Man and Ball Movement	Outside Shooting	Tempo of Attackers	Low Post Action	Size
Normal	Normal	Normal	Stressed	Normal

This attack starts with a guard (1) to guard (2) pass. 2 then dribbles toward the wing on his side (X4) to force coverage by him. Then he passes to 4 who steps out from his low post. As this occurs, 5 rolls to the low *post* and 3 flashes to the open spot in the middle of the zone after X3 has been forced to drop down to cover 5. *(Diagram 5-56)*

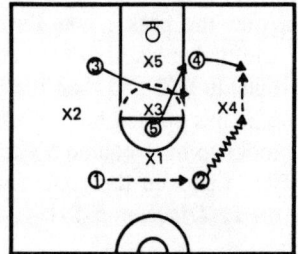

Diagram 5-56

Now 5 may have a quick shot from the *good percentage shooting area* or he may move the ball into 5 or 3 if either has advantage position. 2 and 1 exchange places. *(Diagram 5-57)*

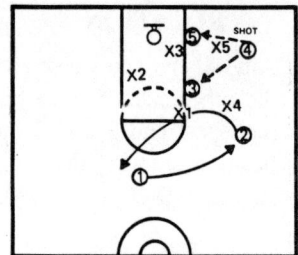

Diagram 5-57

ROTATION

If nothing is possible, 4 passes back out to 1. 3 steps up to the free-throw line, and 5 swings over to a position near the baseline on the other side of the court. *(Diagram 5-58)*

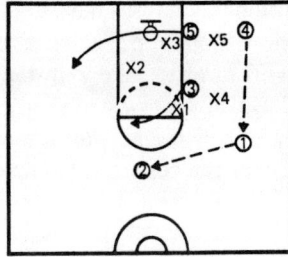

Diagram 5-58

2 now passes to 5. 3 drops to the low-*post*, and 4 comes to the open spot in the middle of the zone. *(Diagram 5-59)*

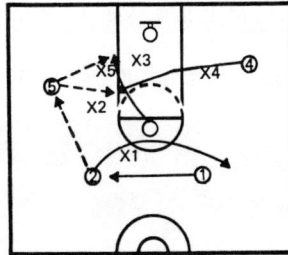

Diagram 5-59

ATTACKING A 1-3-1 ZONE FROM A 2-2-1 ALIGNMENT

Attack number 1

Man and Ball Movement	Outside Shooting	Tempo of Attackers	Low Post Action	Size
Considerable	Necessary	Rapid	Stressed	Normal

The guard on the weak side (2) passes to the wing on that side (4) and cuts through to the corner. 4 passes back out to the other guard (1) who has moved over to fill 2's spot. After the pass, 4 cuts toward the basket head-hunting for a man who might be in position to stop a pass to the low post (either X2 or X3, depending on how the defense reacts). *(Diagram 5-60)*

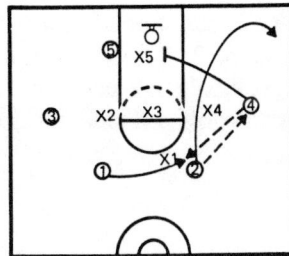

Diagram 5-60

1 quickly returns the ball to the corner, and 2 now looks for 5 coming off 4's *screen*. X5 will have to take 2 in the corner or 2 will have an uncontested shot. X4 has had to stay with 4 while he was at the wing and cannot cover the corner. *(Diagram 5-61)*

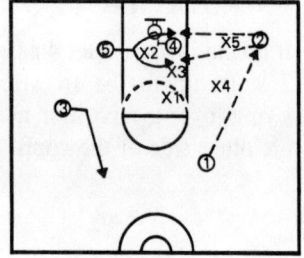

Diagram 5-61

If 2 cannot get the ball inside, he passes back out to 1. 1 moves it across court to 3. 3 then passes to 4 moving out to the corner and cuts through head-hunting. *(Diagram 5-62)*

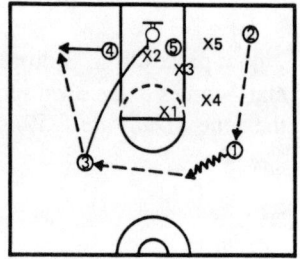

Diagram 5-62

5 comes off 3's *screen* looking for a pass at the low *post*. 1 moves over to the guard spot on the strong side and 2 comes out to the guard spot on the weak side. *(Diagram 5-63)*

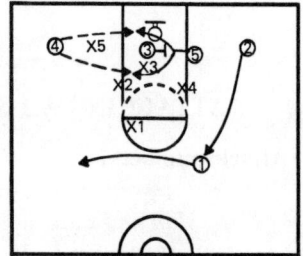

Diagram 5-63

To rotate, 4 passes out to 1 who swings the ball to 2. 3 steps out to the wing spot as 5 goes to the low post and 4 takes the low post on the off-ball side. *(Diagram 5-64)*

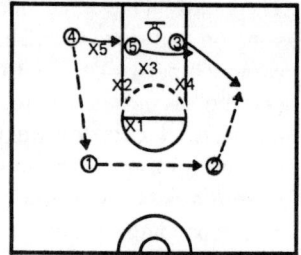

Diagram 5-64

5 now steps out to the corner. After passing
the ball to him, 3 cuts toward the basket
head-hunting for a defensive player. The motion continues this way until a shot occurs.
(Diagram 5-65)

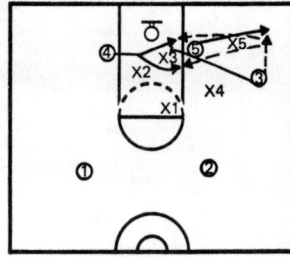

Diagram 5-65

Chapter 6

COACHING AGAINST THE 3-2 ZONE DEFENSE

ATTACKING A 3-2 ZONE FROM A 1-2-2 ALIGNMENT

Attack number 1

Man and Ball Movement	Outside Shooting	Tempo of Attackers	Low Post Action	Size
Limited	Necessary	Normal	Stressed	Normal

To begin this motion a wing (3) moves into a high *post* position. As the pass goes into him from the point man (1), 5 crosses the lane under 4 using him as a *screen*. After 1's pass to 3, he cuts to a wing spot in the area vacated by 3. *(Diagram 6-1)*

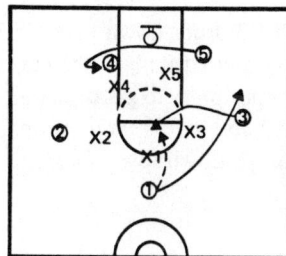

Diagram 6-1

107

If X3 covers 3 at the high post, 1 should dribble the ball to the wing position. *(Diagram 6-2)*

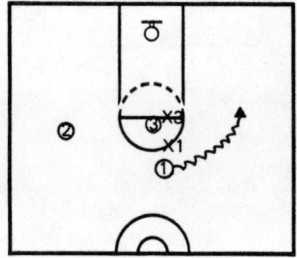

Diagram 6-2

After the ball goes into 3, he may turn and take the shot if he is not covered or look to hit 5 behind 4's screen or to 1 at the wing spot on the other side. *(Diagram 6-3)*

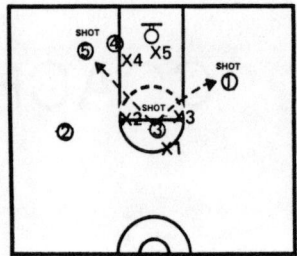

Diagram 6-3

OPTION

5 may also pop to the middle to receive a pass from 1. The wing on his side (3) drops down quickly, expecting a pass from 5. *(Diagram 6-4)*

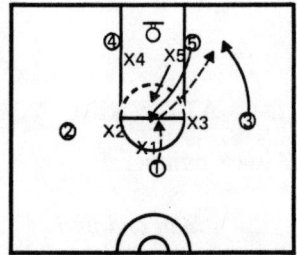

Diagram 6-4

If X3 drops down to cover 3 near the basket, 5 should dribble out to the side looking for an opportunity to get off a quick jump shot from a *good percentage shooting area*. 2 also drops down low. *(Diagram 6-5)*

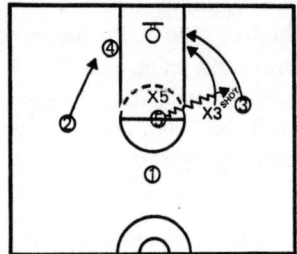

Diagram 6-5

3 continues across the lane providing a *screen* for 4 who pops into the *gap* in the middle and for 2 who goes baseline. 5 can hit either of these men if they are open. *(Diagram 6-6)*

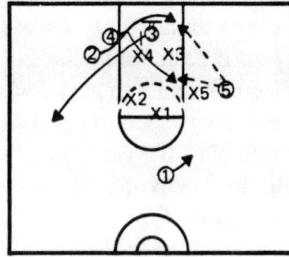

Diagram 6-6

ROTATION

5 passes out to 1. 3 comes to the high *post* in the middle, 4 goes to the low *post* and 2 steps outside. Now we have the same situation as before on the other side. *(Diagram 6-7)*

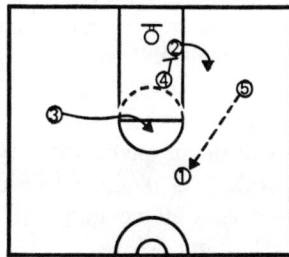

Diagram 6-7

The ball goes to 3 in the middle. If he does not have a shot, he should look to pass to 1 at the wing or to 2 behind 4's *screen*. *(Diagram 6-8)*

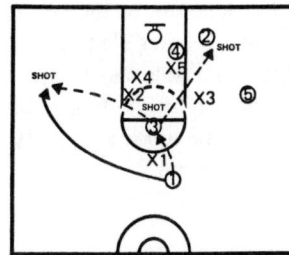

Diagram 6-8

ATTACKING A 3-2 ZONE FROM
A 1-2-2 ALIGNMENT

Attack number 2

Man and Ball Movement	Outside Shooting	Tempo of Attackers	Low Post Action	Size
Normal	Necessary	Normal	Stressed	Normal

The point man passes to the strongside wing (3). 3 immediately looks to hit 2 at the side *post* if he can shut out X1. This would give 2 a quick shot or a pass down to either 4 or 5 at the low *posts* if either X4 or X5 comes up to stop him. If 3 can't hit 2, he looks inside to 5 at the low post if he has advantage position. *(Diagram 6-9)*

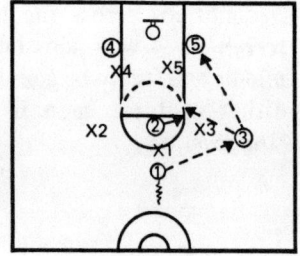

Diagram 6-9

If the ball is passed to 5 at the low post, 2 screens down, head-hunting for anybody (probably X4) who might prevent a pass to 4 who rolls over the top of 2's *screen*. 3 moves into the corner expecting a return pass for a shot or for the opportunity to dump the ball back to 5 if X5 comes out to cover 3. 4 remains at the mid-post on the ball side. *(Diagram 6-10)*

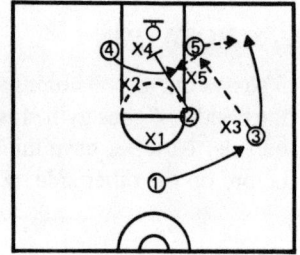

Diagram 6-10

Option. If 5 can't get the ball at the low post, he steps out to the corner to receive a pass from 3. After 3's pass to him, 3 posts low on the ball side as 2 head-hunts for any man who might interfere with a pass to 4 rolling over the *screen*. 1 fills 3's vacated spot. *(Diagram 6-11)*

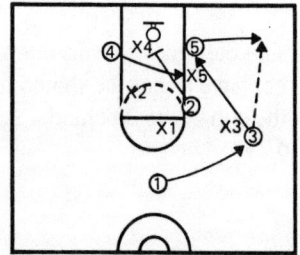

Diagram 6-11

Now 5 may shoot (if X5 does not come out on him quickly) or pass to 3 at the low *post*, 4 at the mid-*post*, or back out to 1 at the wing. *(Diagram 6-12)*

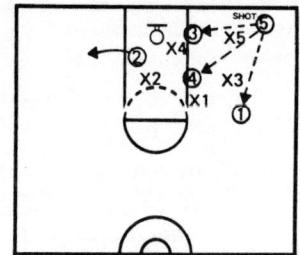

Diagram 6-12

ROTATION

After the pass out to 1, 5 moves back to the low post, 4 comes down and then across to his original low post, 3 comes to the high post at the free throw line and 2 pops out to the wing position. 1 dribbles out to be in position to swing the ball to 2. *(Diagram 6-13)*

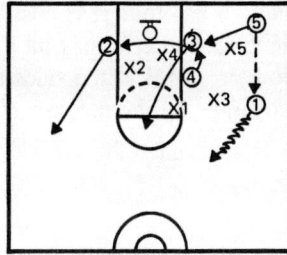

Diagram 6-13

With the ball in 2's hands the same motion is now run again to the other side. *(Diagram 6-14)*

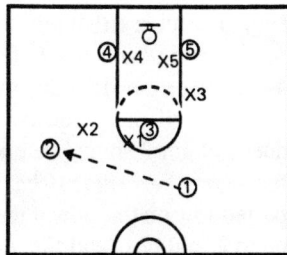

Diagram 6-14

ATTACKING A 3-2 ZONE FROM A 1-3-1 ALIGNMENT

Attack number 1

Man and Ball Movement	Outside Shooting	Tempo of Attackers	Low Post Action	Size
Considerable	Necessary	Normal	Normal	Normal

The front three men are in match up positions. If the ball can be passed to 5 at the high-*post*, it will create problems for the defense. One of the two deep men will have to come up to cover 5. 4 goes to the open spot that is left by the defensive man's coming up to cover 5, and the wing away from that side will drop down quickly to provide a 3-on-2 situation inside. 1 moves to the side to fill the spot vacated by that wing. *(Diagram 6-15)*

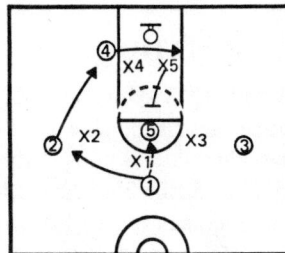

Diagram 6-15

Now 5 has four pass possibilities to players in the *seams*. He may hit either 2 or 4 down low or 1 or 3 at the sides depending on the coverage by the defense. *(Diagram 6-16)*

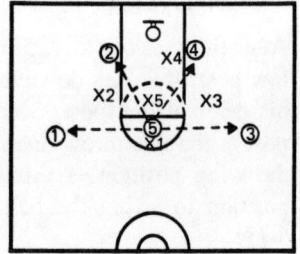

Diagram 6-16

5 is really facing X5 in a 1-on-1 situation. If he does not find anyone open, he should begin a dribble either left or right. As he does so, the wing on that side (3) will drop down to the baseline drawing the defensive man with him. If the defensive man at the wing does not go, 3 should be open at the baseline for a *good percentage shot*. The man who is posted low on the side of the dribble (4) steps up to a mid-*post* and the man at the baseline on the off-ball side (2) comes across to the low-*post*. *(Diagram 6-17)*

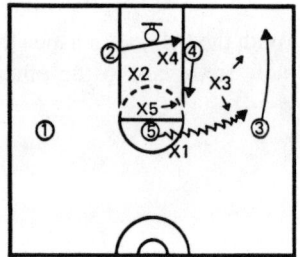

Diagram 6-17

There is a good chance that X5 will not follow 5 all the way and X3 may drop low to cover near the baseline. 5 may shoot if he is open or look to pass to one of the three men (4, 2, or 3) in the *overloaded* situation. 1 comes back out front. *(Diagram 6-18)*

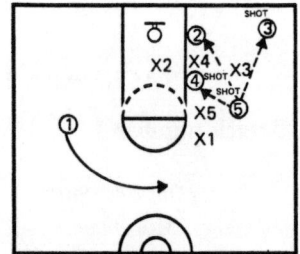

Diagram 6-18

ROTATION

If nothing is open, 5 passes back out to 1. 2 comes across the lane and out to the wing on the other side. 4 pops to the high *post* in the middle. 5 fills 2's vacated low *post* position and 3 comes out to his original wing position. *(Diagram 6-19)*

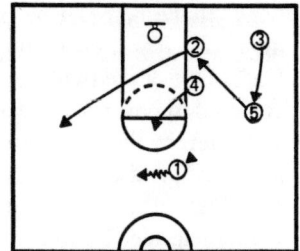

Diagram 6-19

The ball is swung to 2. 4 flashes low and half way out to the corner. 5 comes to the mid-*post* on the ball-side right behind 4's cut. 3 drops down to a low post on the off-ball side. *(Diagram 6-20)*

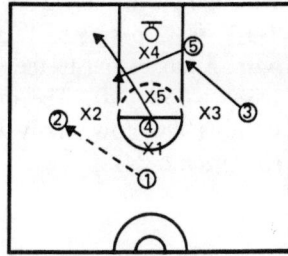

Diagram 6-20

2 may hit 4 in the corner or 5 at the *post* for the quick *percentage shot*. If X3 does not drop back quickly enough, 5 may be able to hit 3 right at the basket for an easy lay-up. *(Diagram 6-21)*

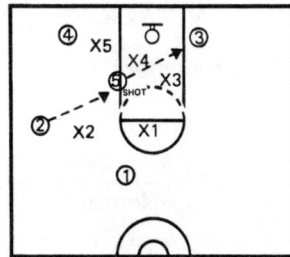

Diagram 6-21

If the ball goes to 4 in the corner, 3 immediately flashes low expecting a pass at the basket as 5 rolls across the lane and down to a *post* position on the off-ball side. If X4 is covering 5 and X3 is late in dropping down to the baseline, 3 may have an easy shot at the basket. *(Diagram 6-22)*

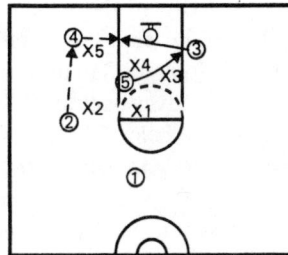

Diagram 6-22

3 does not stay at the low post. If he does not receive an immediate pass, he steps up to the mid-*post* and 5 fills the spot he vacated looking for the same pass at the basket. If neither man is open, 4 throws the ball back out to 2 at the wing. *(Diagram 6-23)*

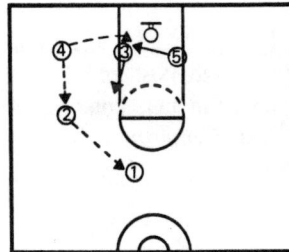

Diagram 6-23

Now the players move back into the original 1-3-1 set. 2 passes to 1. 3 goes to the high *post*. 5 moves out to the wing and 4 establishes a low *post*. The motions and all its options are now ready to be run again. *(Diagram 6-24)*

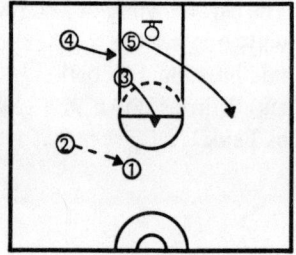

Diagram 6-24

ATTACKING A 3-2 ZONE FROM A 2-1-2 ALIGNMENT

Attack number 1

Man and Ball Movement	Outside Shooting	Tempo of Attackers	Low Post Action	Size
Normal	Necessary	Slow	Stressed	Normal

After a pass from a guard (2) to a wing (5) the guard goes around the man he passes to and into the corner. The wing is playing in a natural *gap* in the zone and he may have a shot if he *penetrates* quickly. If not, he should look for 2 in the corner or 4 at the low *post*. 1 moves over to fill 2's vacated spot. 5 should be below X3 forcing X5 to step up to be able to stop the penetration. With 2 in the corner, X5 will have to recover very rapidly to prevent a shot by him and X4 will have to make a quick adjustment to stop 4 from getting an advantage position on him at the low *post*. *(Diagram 6-25)*

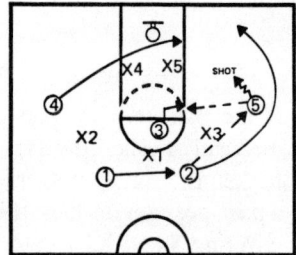

Diagram 6-25

If the pass goes to 2 in the corner, 5 steps to the high post and 1 fills his spot. 2 looks inside in an attempt to get the ball to the low *post*. *(Diagram 6-26)*

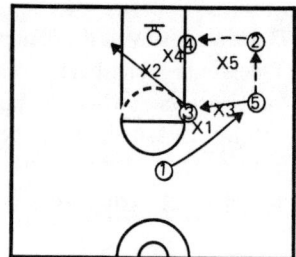

Diagram 6-26

If this cannot be accomplished, 2 passes back out to 1 at the wing and sets a *screen* for 4 to step out behind when the zone begins to flow with the movement of men and the ball to the other side. 1 should take 2 or 3 dribbles to allow the zone to shift before looking back at 4 behind the screen. In the meantime 5 goes to the low post on the weak side and 3 steps out to the wing on that side. *(Diagram 6-27)*

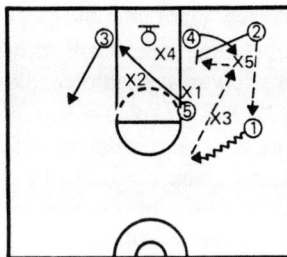

Diagram 6-27

ROTATION

If the pass to 4 is not possible, 1 can pass to 3. As this is happening, 2 comes across the lane under 5's *screen* and out to an open spot, looking for a pass and a quick shot or to dump the ball inside to 5 if he has an advantage position on his man at the low *post*. *(Diagram 6-28)*

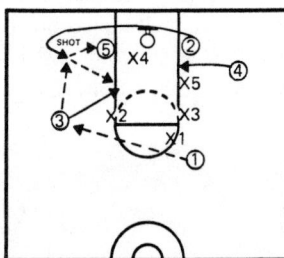

Diagram 6-28

This will continue until the open man gets a shot. 2 passes back out to 1 and sets a crack-down *block* for 5 to step out behind as 3 goes to the low post on the weak side and 4 steps up to a wing spot on that side. *(Diagram 6-29)*

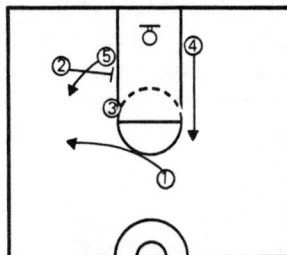

Diagram 6-29

Attack number 2

Man and Ball Movement	Outside Shooting	Tempo of Attackers	Low Post Action	Size
Limited	Normal	Normal	Stressed	Big men

As the guard with the ball (1) approaches the operating area, 3 rolls down the lane, under 4's low post position and out to a deep wing position. 1 can now pass directly to 4 if X4 is not in good position or to 5 if X5 has left him and moved across to help on 4. If neither man is open he will pass to 3 near the corner. *(Diagram 6-30)*

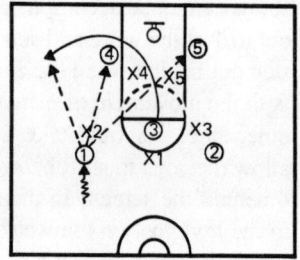

Diagram 6-30

If X4 has not moved out to cover 3, 3 may have a shot. If he has no shot, he may be able to pass inside to 4 at the low *post* if he has advantage position. *(Diagram 6-31)*

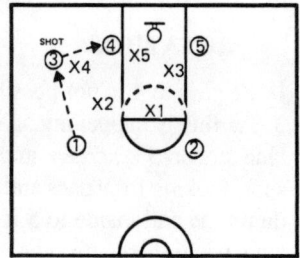

Diagram 6-31

ROTATION

If none of this is possible, 3 passes back out to 1 and moves inside to the low post. 1 swings the ball across to 2 at the other guard spot. 4 crosses under 5's low post and out to a deep wing position. *(Diagram 6-32)*

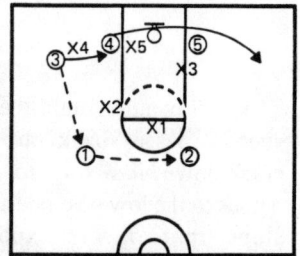

Diagram 6-32

Now the same opportunities exist on this side. 2 must watch the action of both X4 and X5 to know what is open inside. *(Diagram 6-33)*

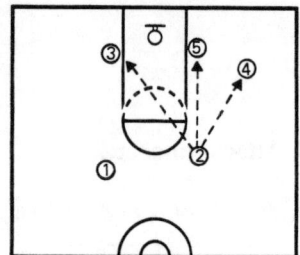

Diagram 6-33

Chapter 7

ATTACKING THE 2-1-2 ZONE DEFENSE

ATTACKING A 2-1-2 ZONE FROM A 1-2-2 ALIGNMENT

Attack number 1

Man and Ball Movement	Outside Shooting	Tempo of Attackers	Low Post Action	Size
Limited	Normal	Normal	Stressed	Normal

The wings are fitted into the *gaps* in this offense, giving them a *good percentage shot* after the first pass. 4 and 5 take a tandem post position near the baseline. The ball is passed to 3 who then makes an effort to *penetrate* at the *seam*. X3 will be forced to come out to stop him. 4 *picks* for 5 forcing

X4 to come across the lane to help out. 2 drops down to the baseline and 1 goes to the top corner of the lane away from the ball. *(Diagram 7-1)*

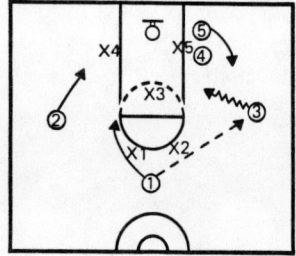

Diagram 7-1

3 may shoot, hit 5 behind the screen, pass to 4 directly inside, lob to 2 at the basket if X4 or X3 does not cover him, or pass back to 1 at the free-throw line. *(Diagram 7-2)*

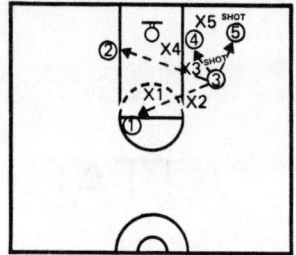

Diagram 7-2

ROTATION

If 1 receives the ball, 2 quickly steps away from the basket expecting a quick pass for the *good percentage shot* as 4 crosses the lane and *posts* low. 5 moves to the low *post* on the off-ball side as 3 goes out to the top corner of the lane. 1 has the same options as was true on the other side. *(Diagram 7-3)*

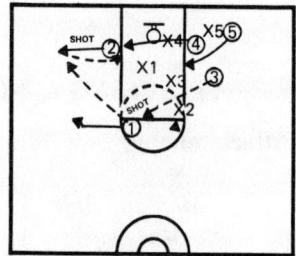

Diagram 7-3

Attack number 2

Man and Ball Movement	Outside Shooting	Tempo of Attackers	Low Post Action	Size
Considerable	Necessary	Slow	Stressed	Normal

The point man (1) dribbles the ball toward one side. The wing on that side (2) drops down and in to the corner. *(Diagram 7-4)*

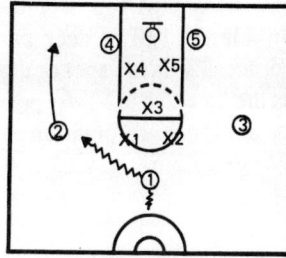

Diagram 7-4

1 passes the ball to 2 in the corner and 2 immediately looks inside to hit 4 at the low *post* or to 5 who has come across the lane and into the *gap* hoping for a pass and a quick jump shot in the *good percentage shooting area*. 3 fills the point spot out front. *(Diagram 7-5)*

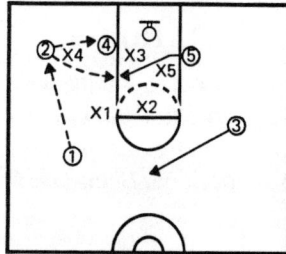

Diagram 7-5

ROTATION

2 passes out to 1 and 1 gets the ball to 3 at the point. After his pass 1 goes diagonally to a mid-*post* position on the other side of the court. 5 moves to a wing spot on the other side of the court. *(Diagram 7-6)*

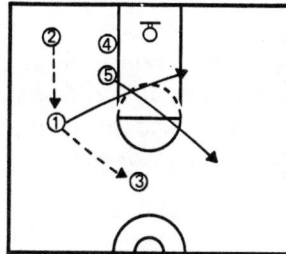

Diagram 7-6

As the ball is being swung to the other side of the court and the defense is sliding in the direction of the flow, 2 steps inside to provide a *screen* for 4 to step behind for a possible return pass. He may have time to get a quick jump shot from the *good percentage shooting area*. 3 must do a good job making it look like he is attempting to swing the ball to the other side. *(Diagram 7-7)*

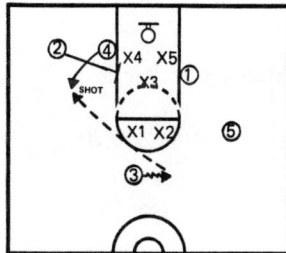

Diagram 7-7

If 3 does pass the ball to 5, 5 attempts to dribble the ball as deep as possible into the corner. 1 fills his spot at the wing as 4 crosses the lane to a low *post* position and 2 comes to a high *post* position on the ball side. *(Diagram 7-8)*

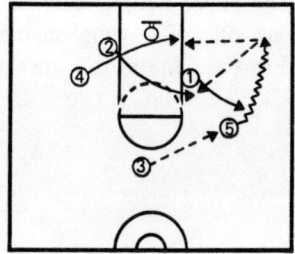

Diagram 7-8

ROTATION

5 passes out to 1 at the wing. 1 then passes to 3 and goes to a mid-*post* position on the other side. 2 moves across the lane and out to a wing position. *(Diagram 7-9)*

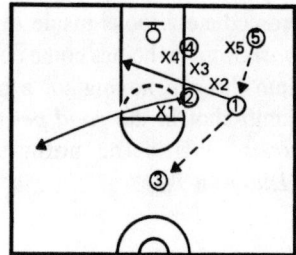

Diagram 7-9

Once again as the defense is sliding with the flow of the offense, 5 sets up a *screen* for 4 to come behind and receive a pass for a quick jump shot. *(Diagram 7-10)*

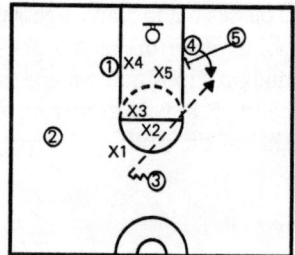

Diagram 7-10

Attack number 3

Man and Ball Movement	Outside Shooting	Tempo of Attackers	Low Post Action	Size
Normal	.Necessary	Rapid	Unstressed	Not major factor

1 begins by passing to a wing (3). 3 then passes the ball to 5 who has moved to the corner from his low *post* position. After his pass, 3 cuts through to the basket under 4 and out to a deep wing spot on the off-ball side. 1 and 2 both move over to be in position to receive a pass and swing the ball to the other side. *(Diagram 7-11)*

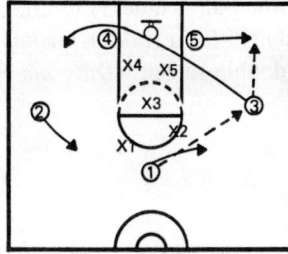

Diagram 7-11

The ball is now passed from 5 to 1 and across to 2. The ball must be swung quickly so that it can reach 3 for a *good percentage shot* behind 4's *screen*. After his pass, 5 moves back to a low *post* on the off-ball side. *(Diagram 7-12)*

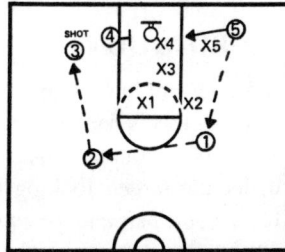

Diagram 7-12

ROTATION

If 3 does not have a shot, he passes back outside to 2. 2 then passes across to 1 as 4 crosses the lane and goes behind 5's *screen* looking for a pass from 1 and a shot from the *good percentage shooting area*. *(Diagram 7-13)*

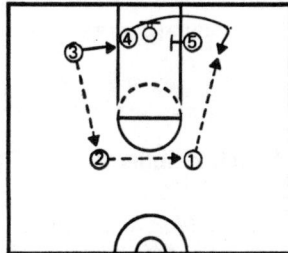

Diagram 7-13

VARIATION

Instead of going to the corner after 1's pass to 3, 5 crosses the lane and goes behind a double *screen* set by 2 and 4. *(Diagram 7-14)*

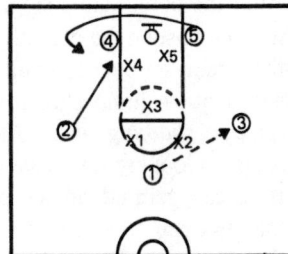

Diagram 7-14

The ball is quickly returned to 1 and he then hits 5 for a *good percentage shot* behind the double *screen*. *(Diagram 7-15)*

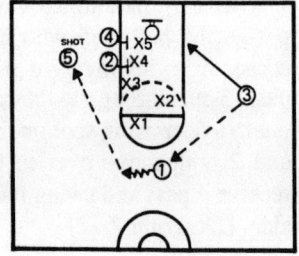

Diagram 7-15

ROTATION

If 5 does not have a shot, he returns the ball to 1. As this is happening, 2 crosses the lane and sets a double *screen* with 3. 4 comes under the *screen* looking for a pass from 1 for a *good percentage shot*. This continues until a shot is taken. 1 should not ignore the man on the weak side because he may be open for a shot as the defense attempts to shift to the other side to stop the shot behind the screen. *(Diagram 7-16)*

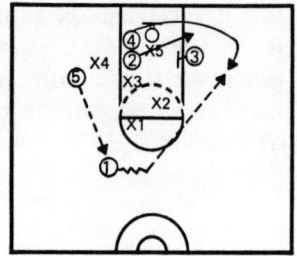

Diagram 7-16

Attack number 4

Man and Ball Movement	Outside Shooting	Tempo of Attackers	Low Post Action	Size
Normal	Necessary	Slow	Stressed	Normal

After the point man's (1) pass to a wing (3), the low post on the off-ball side comes under the screen set by 5 looking for a pass from 3 and a quick jump shot from the *good percentage shooting area*. As he does this, 5 *posts* up looking for a pass either from 3 or 4 if he can gain advantage position. 1 moves into an open area near the free-throw line. 2 fills 1's vacated spot. *(Diagram 7-17)*

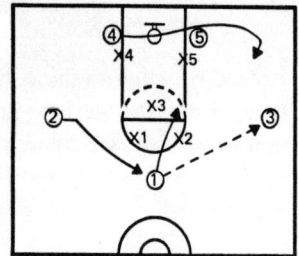

Diagram 7-17

The *overload* has now been accomplished. 3 is in the *seam* of the zone and may have a shot before a defensive player can get to him. The defense must now make several critical adjustments. X2 must get over to stop 3's shot; X5 must fight over the screen and prevent a shot by 4; X4 must not allow 5 to gain an advantage position on him at the low post. If X3 drops back to help inside, 1 may be open for a pass and a quick jump shot by *penetrating* the open spot in the middle. He would need to shut out X1 to have an advantage position. *(Diagram 7-18)*

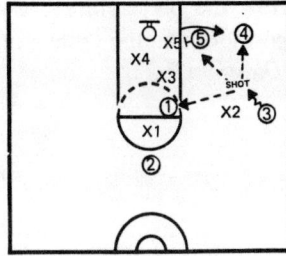

Diagram 7-18

If none of this materializes, 3 passes back to 2 and goes to the corner on the other side. 1 steps out to a wing position and 4 *screens* down for 5. *(Diagram 7-19)*

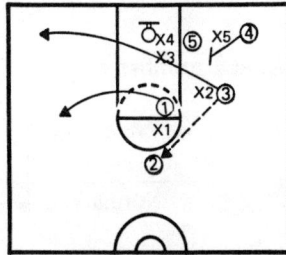

Diagram 7-19

2 now has a choice of hitting 5 who has come counter flow out behind 4's *screen*, passing to 4 at the low *post* if the defense is not in correct position, or swinging the ball to 1 at the wing. If he passes to 1 he follows his pass after 1 hits 3 in the corner. If the ball is moved quickly enough, 3 may have a shot in the corner. If not, he should look for 4 at the low *post* or 1 in the opening near the corner of the key. *(Diagram 7-20)*

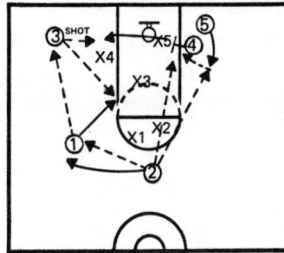

Diagram 7-20

3 looks to hit 4 rolling across to a low post or to 1 at the high post. If he cannot pass to either man, the ball is moved back to 2. 2 then passes to 1 stepping out to the point. 3 goes across the middle to the wing on the other side. *(Diagram 7-21)*

Diagram 7-21

Now the players are back in their original positions and the same motion begins again. *(Diagram 7-22)*

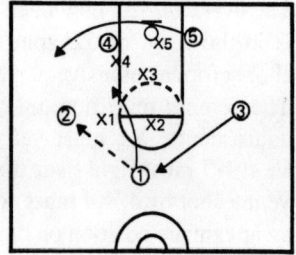

Diagram 7-22

Attack number 5

Man and Ball Movement	Outside Shooting	Tempo of Attackers	Low Post Action	Size
Normal	Necessary	Normal	Stressed	Normal

From a double stack low, the baseline man on one side (5) pops out to a wing to receive a pass from 1. 2 comes across the lane and into the strongside corner. *(Diagram 7-23)*

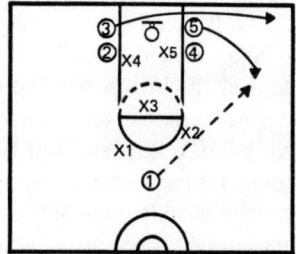

Diagram 7-23

Now 5 may dump the ball into 4 at the low *post* or pass it to 3 in the corner. In this triangle, any man may be open if the defense adjusts improperly. *(Diagram 7-24)*

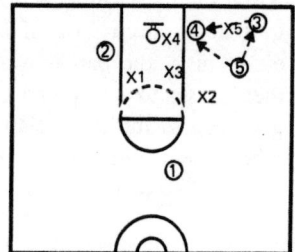

Diagram 7-24

If nothing is open, 5 passes back out to 1 and he and 3 *screen* down for 4 to step behind for a pass and a shot in the *good percentage shooting area*. Before making the pass to 4, 1 should start a dribble to the other side to get the zone shifting. 2 steps up to be in position to receive a pass. *(Diagram 7-25)*

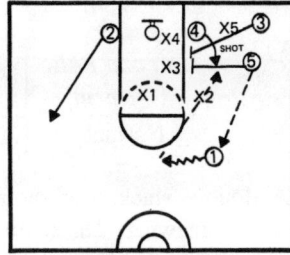

Diagram 7-25

After 1 passes to 2, 3 and 5 cross, 3 going to the wing and 5 going to the corner. 4 comes across to the strongside low *post*. *(Diagram 7-26)*

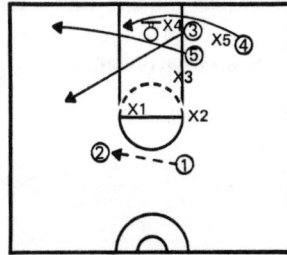

Diagram 7-26

2 passes to 3 at the wing and again we have a triangle to take advantage of defensive misplay. 1 drops down into off-side rebounding position. *(Diagram 7-27)*

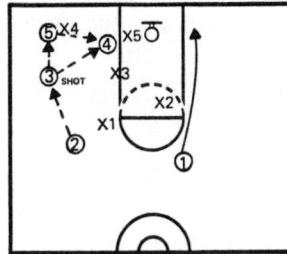

Diagram 7-27

Again, after a pass back out to the point, a double *screen* is set for 4 to shoot behind. *(Diagram 7-28)*

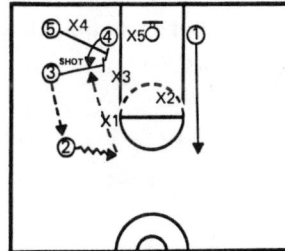

Diagram 7-28

Attack number 6

Man and Ball Movement	Outside Shooting	Tempo of Attackers	Low Post Action	Size
Normal	Necessary	Normal	Stressed	Normal

A double stack low should compress the zone somewhat. The bottom men (2 and 3) move out to a wing position and the point man may hit either man. As he does so the top man on the other side comes to a high *post* near the free-throw line and the wing on the off-ball side drops back down in *rebounding* position. *(Diagram 7-29)*

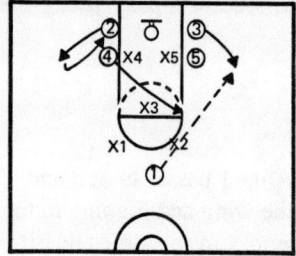

Diagram 7-29

3 should be playing in a *seam* and may have a shot if he isn't covered quickly. He looks to pass the ball to 5 at the low *post* if he has advantage position or to 4 at the high post. *(Diagram 7-30)*

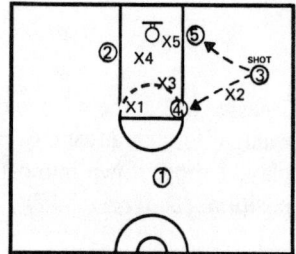

Diagram 7-30

If 5 isn't open low, he will move out to the corner and 4 will drop down to his low *post*. *(Diagram 7-31)*

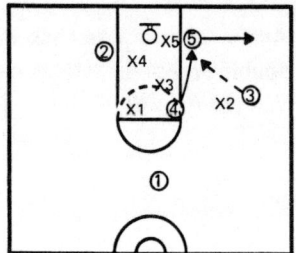

Diagram 7-31

3 now hits 5 in the corner and cuts through to the other wing's spot. 1 fills his vacated spot. 2 now comes to the open spot at a side *post* on the strong side. An *overload* has now been affected. *(Diagram 7-32)*

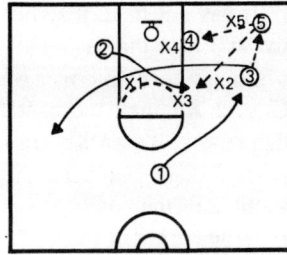

Diagram 7-32

ROTATION

5 passes out to 1 and moves in to set a *screen* for 2 to come under and out to a deep wing position. 4 crosses the lane and takes a low post. 1 starts a dribble to the point. He may come back counter flow or he may swing the ball to 3 to start the same motion on the other side. If he comes back with a pass to 2, 2 may have a shot or begin the motion again on his side. *(Diagram 7-33)*

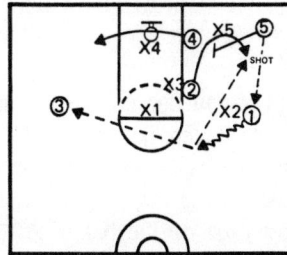

Diagram 7-33

ATTACKING A 2-1-2 ZONE FROM A 1-3-1 ALIGNMENT

Attack number 1

Man and Ball Movement	Outside Shooting	Tempo of Attackers	Low Post Action	Size
Considerable	Necessary	Rapid	Normal	Normal

The attack begins with a pass from 1 to a wing man. The pass is returned to him immediately. While this is happening, the other wing man is moving up into a position to provide a screen for the point after he receives the pass. 1 then comes to the side where the screen is set, using it to enable him to *penetrate* the zone as deeply as possible looking for the *good percentage shot*. 4 moves into the corner on the ball side and 5 drops down to a low *post* position. After 3 returns the ball to 1, he moves down toward the basket on the off-ball side. *(Diagram 7-34)*

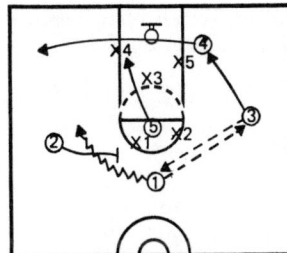

Diagram 7-34

If 1 does not have the shot, he should look first at 3 near the basket on the off-ball side. In a hurry to help cover on the strong side, X3 and X5 may momentarily ignore 3. A high pass at the basket could lead to an easy score. 1 may also hit either 4 or 5 in their positions if they are open. 4 can either shoot from the corner or dump the ball into 5 at the post. *(Diagram 7-35)*

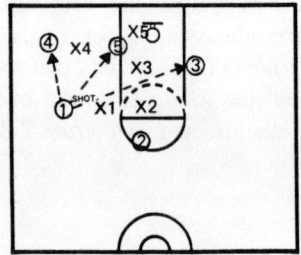

Diagram 7-35

If none of this is possible, the ball is passed out to 2 who then uses a *pick* by 3 in the same manner as 1 had used it on the other side. 4 goes to the other corner and 5 moves to the low *post* on the ball side. 1 drops down to look for a pass at the basket. *(Diagram 7-36)*

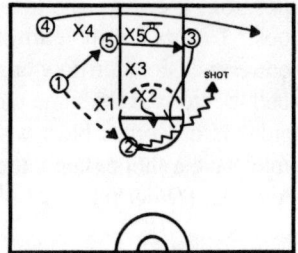

Diagram 7-36

2 now has the same pass possibilities as was true on the other side. 1 should be watched carefully because the defense may fail to cover him in their hurry to shift to the other side. *(Diagram 7-37)*

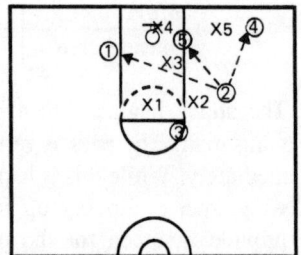

Diagram 7-37

Attack number 2

Man and Ball Movement	Outside Shooting	Tempo of Attackers	Low Post Action	Size
Normal	Normal	Normal	Stressed	Normal

1 passes to the wing on the weak side (2). As this happens, 3 rolls to the low *post* in an attempt to get advantage position. 5 flashes to the open spot near the mid-*post* area. 4 drops down to fill 5's vacated spot. *(Diagram 7-38)*

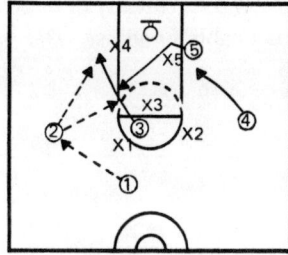

Diagram 7-38

If 2 hits 3 at the low post he will move into the corner. 5 makes a move into the lane away from the coverage by X3. If X5 comes across to help out, 5 can flip 4 a pass at the bucket. With 2 in the corner, this puts pressure on the defense to cover three baseline men along with 5 in the middle. *(Diagram 7-39)*

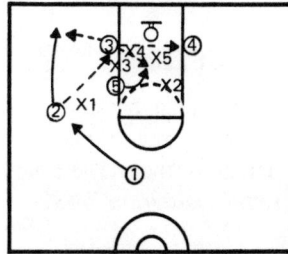

Diagram 7-39

ROTATION

To rotate, 3 passes out to 2 in the corner and then goes to the high post on the other side. 5 rolls to the low post on that side and 4 steps out to receive a swing pass from 1 who has taken the pass from 2 in the corner. *(Diagram 7-40)*

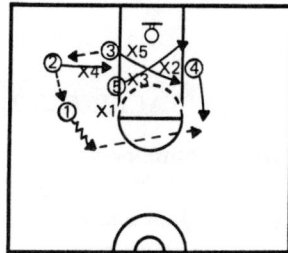

Diagram 7-40

OPTION

If 2 can pass to 5 in the middle, he will *screen* down for 3 to step out behind for a pass and a shot in the *good percentage shooting area*. 1 goes to the wing on the weak side to give 5 four pass possibilities. *(Diagram 7-41)*

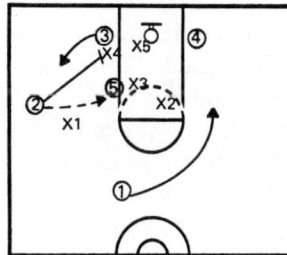

Diagram 7-41

Now 5 can hit any of these men if the defense is unable to adjust. *(Diagram 7-42)*

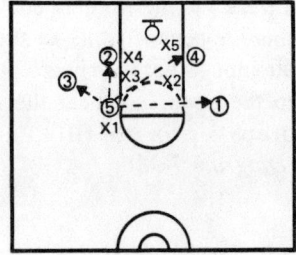

Diagram 7-42

OPTION

Rather than passing inside, 2 may dribble into the corner to place stress on the baseline defensive men. The rotation will remain the same. *(Diagram 7-43)*

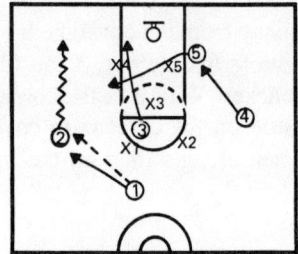

Diagram 7-43

ATTACKING A 2-1-2 ZONE FROM A 2-1-2 ALIGNMENT

Attack number 1

Man and Ball Movement	Outside Shooting	Tempo of Attackers	Low Post Action	Size
Considerable	Normal	Rapid	Stressed	Normal

A guard (2) starts by dribbling into the gap between the front two defensive men. The other guard (1) goes behind to receive a flip pass and in turn pass to 5 at the wing. This should leave a *gap* for 5 to get a jump shot if the defense cannot adjust. Hopefully, X5 has had to come out a bit. 3 moves down to get off-side rebounding position. *(Diagram 7-44)*

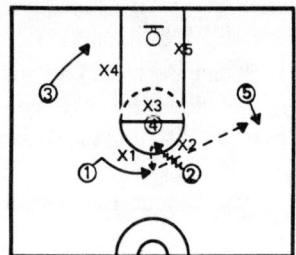

Diagram 7-44

After 1 passes to 5 he goes around him into the corner. 4 rolls to the low *post* hoping to get advantage position and a pass. *(Diagram 7-45)*

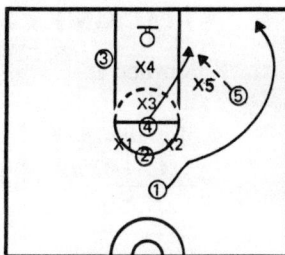

Diagram 7-45

After 4 goes to the low post, 3 pops up into the open spot near the high post on the strong side. If the ball goes to 1 in the corner, he may have a shot or he may be able to dump it into 4 at the low *post*. *(Diagram 7-46)*

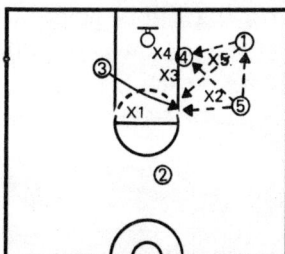

Diagram 7-46

ROTATION

If none of this develops, 5 passes back to 2 at the point. As 5 passes out, 4 rolls across the lane and then out to the wing. 3 moves to the strong side low *post*. 1 rotates across to the other corner and 5 flashes down and then up to the open spot near the high *post*. *(Diagram 7-47)*

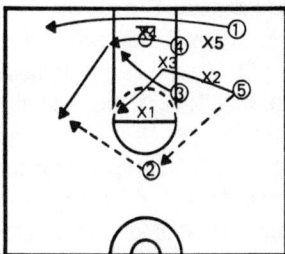

Diagram 7-47

4 passes to 1 in the corner. Again, he may have a shot or the ball may be moved to 3 at the low *post* or to 5 at the high *post* if either is open. *(Diagram 7-48)*

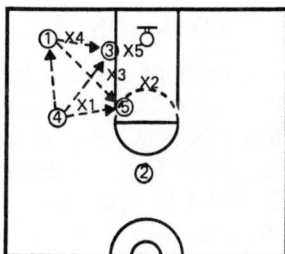

Diagram 7-48

ATTACKING A 2-1-2 ZONE FROM A 2-3 ALIGNMENT

Attack number 1

Man and Ball Movement	Outside Shooting	Tempo of Attackers	Low Post Action	Size
Normal	Normal	Rapid	Stressed	Normal

A guard (1) passes to the wing on his side (3). Immediately the wing is in the *gap* and possibly open for a *good percentage shot*. X4 will be pulled out to cover him. 5 rolls to the low *post* on the ball side and 4 comes to the high *post* on the same side. *(Diagram 7-49)*

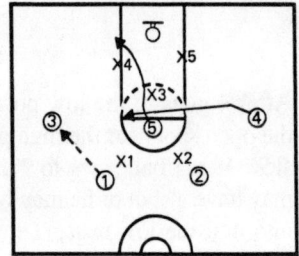

Diagram 7-49

3 should attempt to hit 4 at the *post*. As this is happening, 2 moves down to a low *post* on the off-ball side and 1 fills the spot vacated by 2. Now 4 can look inside at the two men posted low. It may be that X4 will not be able to get back or X5 will not be able to recover and stop 2 near the basket. A direct pass to either of the two should lead to a muscle shot at the basket. He also has a chance for a *good percentage shot* if X3 cannot cover him quickly. *(Diagram 7-50)*

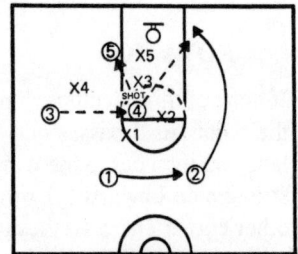

Diagram 7-50

ROTATION

If 4 can't hit either man, he flips the ball back out to 1 and goes to the low *post* on the ball side as 2 pops out to the wing on the same side. 5 quickly flashes to the high *post*. 2 should be open for a pass at the wing. *(Diagram 7-51)*

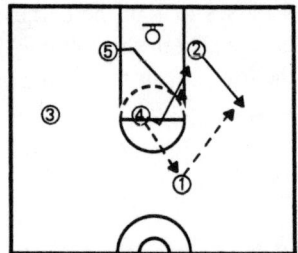

Diagram 7-51

The same possibilities now exist again. 2 may pass inside to 4 or directly to 5 at the post. 5 may shoot or pass to either 4 or 3 at the low *posts*. *(Diagram 7-52)*

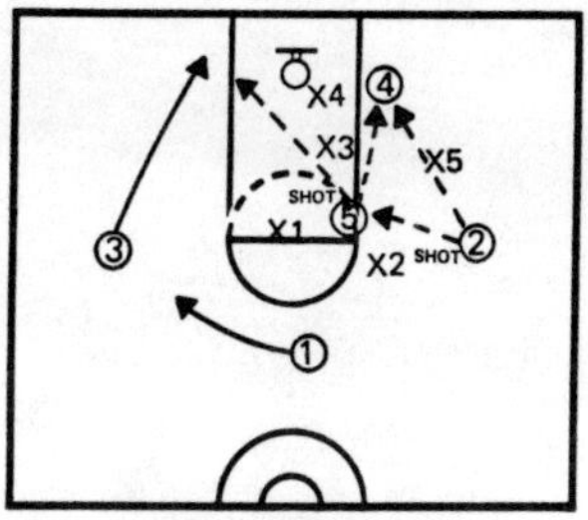

Diagram 7-52

Chapter 8

HOW TO DEFEAT THE 2-3 ZONE DEFENSE

ATTACKING A 2-3 ZONE FROM A 1-2-2 ALIGNMENT

Attack number 1

Man and Ball Movement	Outside Shooting	Tempo of Attackers	Low Post Action	Size
Normal	Necessary	Rapid	Normal	Normal

1 passes to a wing (3) and goes behind him to receive a return pass. After the return pass 3 cuts to the low *post* on the off-ball side as 4 comes to the high *post* on the ball side. 5 moves to the corner and 2 fills the spot vacated by 1. *(Diagram 8-1)*

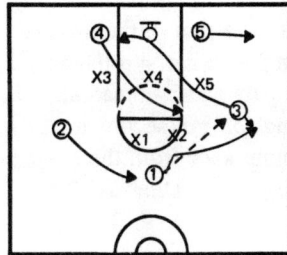

Diagram 8-1

1 looks to hit 4 coming to the *gap* in the zone for a quick jump shot. If he is not open, 1 passes out to 2 at the point. 2 now hits 3 coming up to the free-throw line extended. 5 cross over into the corner on the ball side. *(Diagram 8-2)*

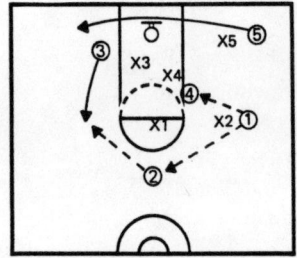

Diagram 8-2

4 rolls across the lane into the *gap* looking for a pass from 3. If he is not open, 3 passes to 5 in the corner. 1 moves down to an off-side rebounding position. *(Diagram 8-3)*

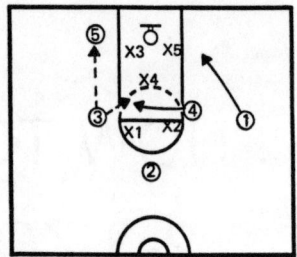

Diagram 8-3

If 3 hits 5, then 4 rolls to the basket expecting a pass. *(Diagram 8-4)*

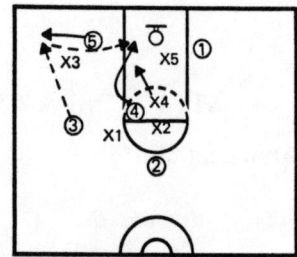

Diagram 8-4

If, as a part of the original set, 1 passes to 5 in the corner, 4 rolls to the basket looking for a pass and 3 immediately fills his spot at the high *post* expecting a pass from 5 for a quick jump shot from the *good percentage shooting area*. *(Diagram 8-5)*

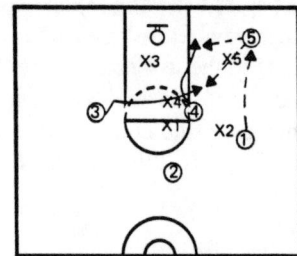

Diagram 8-5

ROTATION

5 passes back out to 1. The ball is then swung from 1 to 2 and then to 4 who has come out to the wing position from a spot near the basket. 5 moves to the other corner and 3 crosses the lane to the high *post* on the ball side. The players are now in position to begin the motion again on the other side. *(Diagram 8-6)*

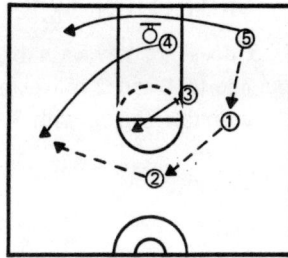

Diagram 8-6

Attack number 2

Man and Ball Movement	Outside Shooting	Tempo of Attackers	Low Post Action	Size
Limited	Necessary	Rapid	Unstressed	Not major factor

The motion begins with a pass from the point to a wing (3). The other wing (2) drops down and sets a double *screen* with the low post (4) on his side. *(Diagram 8-7)*

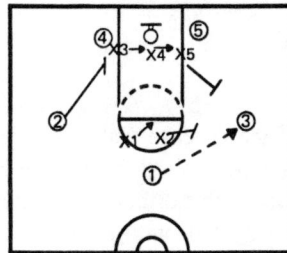

Diagram 8-7

3 passes back to 1. As this is happening, 5 crosses the lane and goes under the double *screen* set by 4 and 2 looking for a pass from 1 for a *good percentage shot*. *(Diagram 8-8)*

Diagram 8-8

ROTATION

If 5 does not have a shot, he passes back
outside to 1 and 2 moves across the lane to
set a double screen with 3. *(Diagram 8-9)*

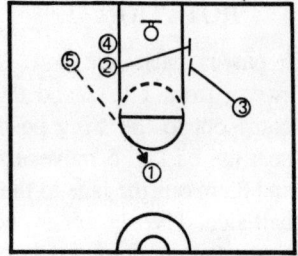

Diagram 8-9

Now 4 crosses the lane and goes under the
double *screen* looking for the pass from 1.
(Diagram 8-10)

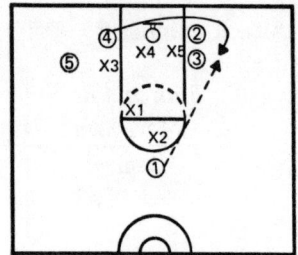

Diagram 8-10

If the defense makes a quick adjustment on
this rotation, 1 may come back to the weak
side with a dribble and a shot behind a *screen*
set by 5 or with a pass to 5 at the high post
followed by a move behind him looking for a
return pass and a shot behind his *screen*.
(Diagram 8-11)

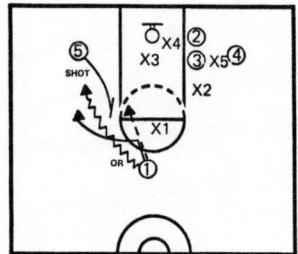

Diagram 8-11

Attack number 3

Man and Ball Movement	Outside Shooting	Tempo of Attackers	Low Post Action	Size
Considerable	Necessary	Rapid	Stressed	Normal

1 begins the attack with a pass to a wing (5). 5 then passes to 4 who has moved to the corner. 3 comes to the strong side high *post* as 2 drops down to take a low *post* on the off-ball side. *(Diagram 8-12)*

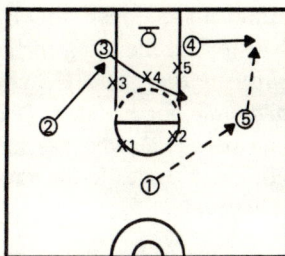

Diagram 8-12

X5 must move out quickly to cover 4 in the corner. From this *overload*, 5 cuts through to the basket after his pass to the corner and out to the wing on the other side. 4 may hit 5 cutting through, 3 at the *high* post or 2 who crosses the lane to the low *post*. None of this is likely. The real opportunities now come on the rotation. *(Diagram 8-13)*

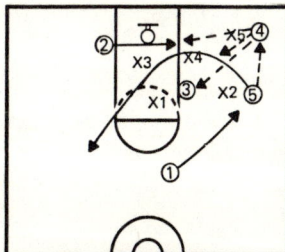

Diagram 8-13

ROTATION

4 passes outside to 1 and moves to a low *post* on top of 2. 3 returns to his original low *post* position. *(Diagram 8-14)*

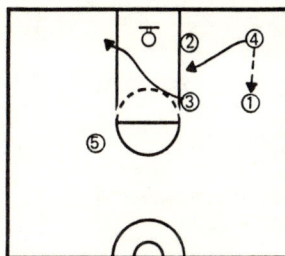

Diagram 8-14

As the ball is being swung to the other side, 4 and 2 hold their spots. 2 pops out behind 4's *screen* and looks for a pass from 1 and a *good percentage shot*. This occurs as the defense is sliding in the other direction with the flow. This movement gives the offense the advantage of being able to go in either direction. If a defensive man holds and tries to fight around or through the *screen*, 1 may throw the ball directly to 4 at the low post. *(Diagram 8-15)*

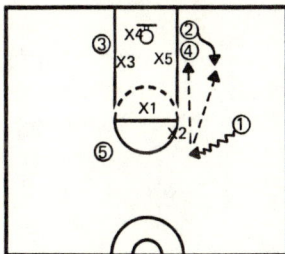

Diagram 8-15

Another great possibility is that 1 can get the ball to 5 at the wing for a *good percentage shot* in the *gap*. He should attempt to *penetrate* for his shot. If he is covered, he can pass to 3 who has moved out into the corner. 4 comes to the strongside high *post*. *(Diagram 8-16)*

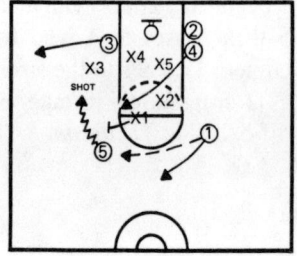

Diagram 8-16

The same motion now occurs again on this side. *(Diagram 8-17)*

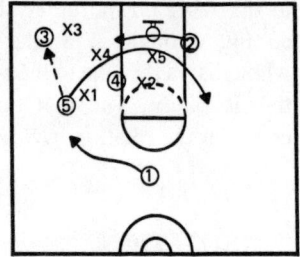

Diagram 8-17

Attack number 4

Man and Ball Movement	Outside Shooting	Tempo of Attackers	Low Post Action	Size
Normal	Necessary	Normal	Stressed	Normal

1 passes to a wing (3) and goes to a high *post* position under X2 looking for a return pass. While this is happening, 5 moves to the corner and 2 moves over to fill 1's vacated spot. *(Diagram 8-18)*

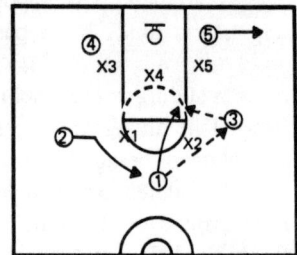

Diagram 8-18

If 3 does not hit 1, he then looks to pass to 5 in the corner. After the pass he moves to a low *post* on the strong side. As soon as 1 sees the ball passed to the corner, he moves to a spot in the *gap* between 5 in the corner and 4 at the low post. *(Diagram 8-19)*

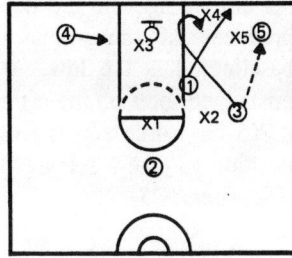

Diagram 8-19

5 then dribbles into the *gap* between X5 and X2, looking to draw them to him and create an opening for one of the inside men. If he draws X5 with him, either 1 or 3 may be open depending on how X4 plays it. If X3 steps across to help, 4 may be open at the basket on the off-ball side. If none of this is open, he can pass back out to 2 at the point. *(Diagram 8-20)*

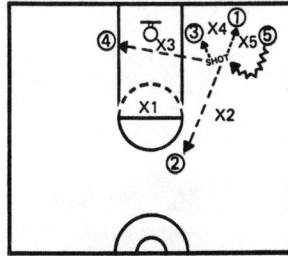

Diagram 8-20

ROTATION

After 2 receives the pass at the point, he quickly swings it to 4 who has stepped out to a wing position from the low post. 2 then moves to the high *post* position under X1 as 3 moves quickly across the lane and out into the corner on the ball side. 5 steps out to take the point position vacated by 2. *(Diagram 8-21)*

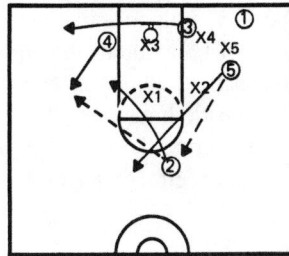

Diagram 8-21

The same action now occurs on this side of the court. 4 passes to 3 in the corner and moves to a low *post* position as 2 goes to the *gap* near the baseline. *(Diagram 8-22)*

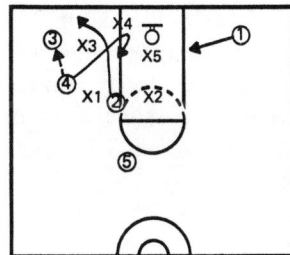

Diagram 8-22

3's dribble into the gap between X3 and X1 produces the same opportunities: 2 at the baseline, 4 at the low *post* if he is being misplayed, or 1 on the off-ball side low *post* if X5 has come across to help out. 5 is in position to take a release pass at the point. *(Diagram 8-23)*

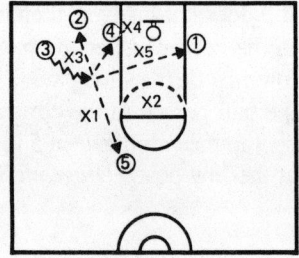

Diagram 8-23

ATTACKING A 2-3 ZONE FROM A 1-3-1 ALIGNMENT

Attack number 1

Man and Ball Movement	Outside Shooting	Tempo of Attackers	Low Post Action	Size
Considerable	Necessary	Normal	Normal	Normal

Point man 1 passes to a wing (3). The high post (5) rolls to a low *post* as 4 comes from the off-ball side to the corner on the side of the ball. 2 angles in and then across to the strongside high *post*. In this *overload* 3 may hit either 2, 5, or 4 if he does not have the shot himself. *(Diagram 8-24)*

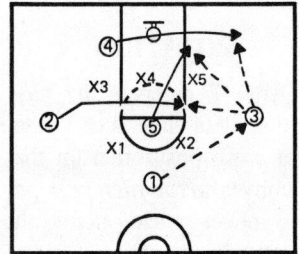

Diagram 8-24

If 3 passes the ball to 2 in the *gap*, a quick jump shot may follow a short dribble out of the crowd. 2 may also pass to either 4 or 5 near the baseline if X4 or X5 converge on him. *(Diagram 8-25)*

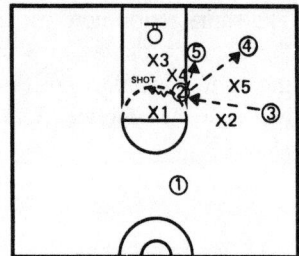

Diagram 8-25

If 3 passes to 4 in the corner, he will cut through toward the basket looking for a return pass near the basket. If he does not receive the pass, he continues through and out to the wing on the off-ball side. 4 should look to dump the ball into 5 at the low *post*. 1 fills 3's vacated spot and 2 takes the point. *(Diagram 8-26)*

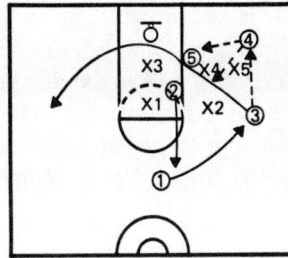

Diagram 8-26

ROTATION

The ball is swung from 4 to 1 to 2 and across to 3 on the other side. 4 moves to the corner on the other side and 5 comes to the high *post*. *(Diagram 8-27)*

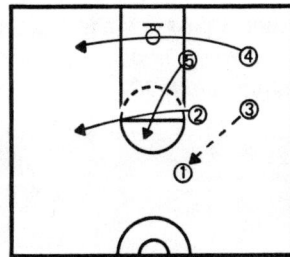

Diagram 8-27

If 4 is not open in the corner, 3 can pass back out to 1. 4 then goes to the opposite corner, 5 comes to the high *post*, and 2 moves to the wing on the other side. *(Diagram 8-28)*

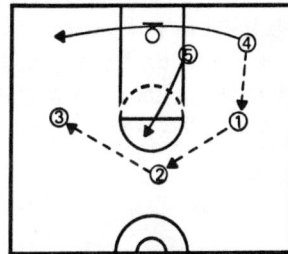

Diagram 8-28

Attack number 2

Man and Ball Movement	Outside Shooting	Tempo of Attackers	Low Post Action	Size
Limited	Necessary	Normal	Normal	Normal

1 passes to the wing on the strong side (2) hoping to commit X1 to him. 5 steps up into the open spot in the middle of the zone as 3 drops to the low *post* on the strong side in an attempt to get advantage position. 1 moves away from his pass. *(Diagram 8-29)*

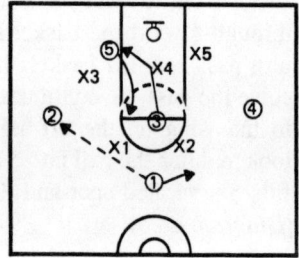

Diagram 8-29

If 2 can make the pass to 5, 5 may have a shot, a pass down to 4 at the low *post*, to 4 at the wing under X2, or to 2 under X1. *(Diagram 8-30)*

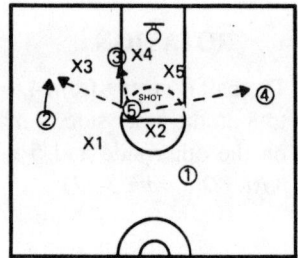

Diagram 8-30

ROTATION

If none of these passes is possible, 5 flips the ball out to 1. 1 passes down to 4 at the wing as 5 rolls to the strongside low *post* and 4 comes into the open spot in the middle of the zone. *(Diagram 8-31)*

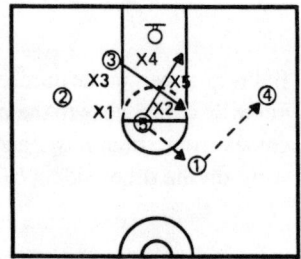

Diagram 8-31

Now the same opportunities exist again. After 4 gets the ball to 3, 3 may shoot, pass down to 5 at the low *post*, or to 2 or 4 underneath the defensive guards. *(Diagram 8-32)*

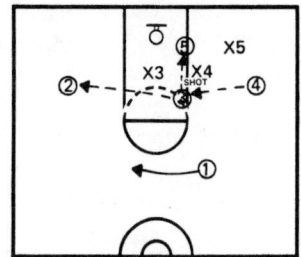

Diagram 8-32

ATTACKING A 2-3 ZONE FROM A 2-1-2 ALIGNMENT

Attack number 1

Man and Ball Movement	Outside Shooting	Tempo of Attackers	Low Post Action	Size
Limited	Necessary	Normal	Unstressed	Not a major factor

This attack stresses *quick shots at the seams*. Guard 2 passes to guard 1 and then goes to the corner on the ball side. 5 moves over to the top corner of the key on the ball side. *(Diagram 8-33)*

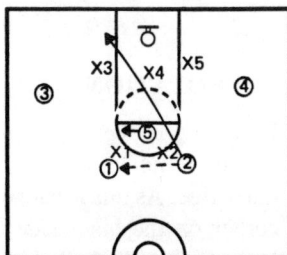

Diagram 8-33

At this point 1 may be able to hit 5 at the high *post* as X1 moves out on him. Several players are fitted into gaps and after 5 turns to the basket he should look to hit one of them or take the shot if he is not challenged by X4. *(Diagram 8-34)*

Diagram 8-34

With 2 near the basket at the baseline and 3 at the wing, it is difficult for X3 to cover both men. 4 should watch X5. If he goes into the lane to help out he can move down toward the basket expecting a pass from 5. Essentially, 5 needs to watch the play of X3 and X5 and adjust his actions to their play. *(Diagram 8-35)*

Diagram 8-35

If the ball is passed to 3, 2 goes out to the corner on the ball side. After the pass to 2 in the corner, 5 rolls to the basket looking for a pass and 4 fills the mid-*post* position looking for a pass and a *quick shot from a good percentage area*. 5 continues on through and out to the wing on the other side. *(Diagram 8-36)*

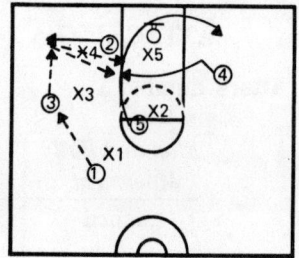

Diagram 8-36

ROTATION

If nothing is open, the ball is swung from 2 to 3 to 1 and across to 5 at the wing on the other side. As this is happening, 2 goes to the corner on the other side and 4 rolls to the high post on the ball side. *(Diagram 8-37)*

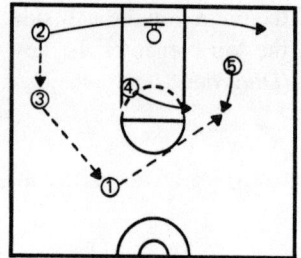

Diagram 8-37

Same opportunities again. If 5 does not have a shot in his new *gap*, he passes to the corner. 4 rolls through and out to the other side and 3 fills at the mid-*post* on the ball side. *(Diagram 8-38)*

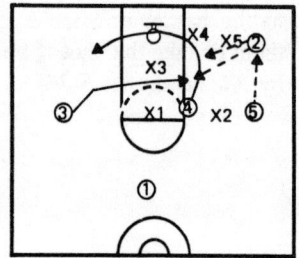

Diagram 8-38

Attack number 2

Man and Ball Movement	Outside Shooting	Tempo of Attackers	Low Post Action	Size
Normal	Necessary	Normal	Normal	Normal

5 takes a side post set. The offense may
begin to either side. In the diagram, 1 passes
to 2 and then moves to a wing position on the
ball side. 4 goes to the corner and 3 then
moves to the low *post* position on the ball
side. 5 comes across to take the same *post*
position on the other side. *(Diagram 8-39)*

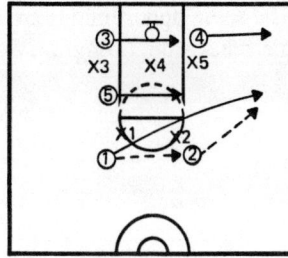

Diagram 8-39

1 is now in a natural *gap* and may take the
shot if he is open, or he may look to hit either
5, 4, or 3. *(Diagram 8-40)*

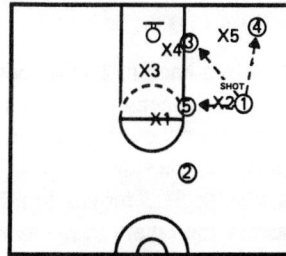

Diagram 8-40

If 1 passes to 4 in the corner, he cuts toward
the basket looking for a quick return pass. If
he does not receive it, he continues through
and back out to a guard position in front on
the off-ball side. 5 steps out and fills the spot
vacated by 1. He may also dump the ball
inside to 3 at the low *post*. *(Diagram 8-41)*

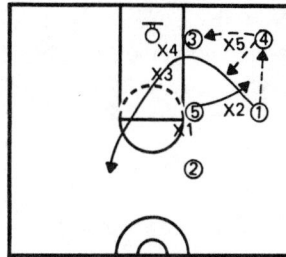

Diagram 8-41

4 then passes back outside to 5 who in turn
passes to 2. After the pass, 5 goes back to the
side *post* position. 2 passes to 1 and goes to
the wing on the other side. 3 goes to the
corner on the opposite side and 4 moves to
the low *post* on the ball side. *(Diagram 8-42)*

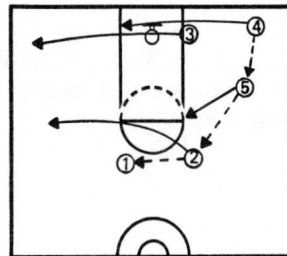

Diagram 8-42

The same opportunities are now available on the other side. *(Diagram 8-43)*

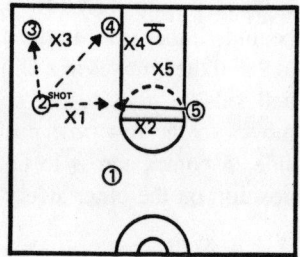

Diagram 8-43

ROTATION

4 passes back to 1 and goes to the low *post*. As this happens, 5 goes out to the guard spot in front on the off-ball side. 1 passes to 2 and moves to the side *post* position. 2 then passes across to 5. 3 moves to a low *post* position across the lane. *(Diagram 8-44)*

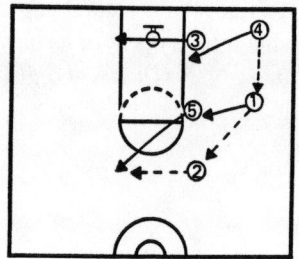

Diagram 8-44

Now the players are in position to start the same motion on the other side. *(Diagram 8-45)*

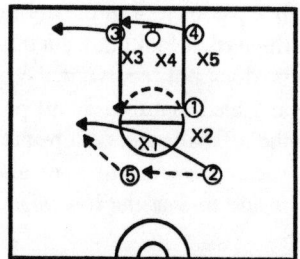

Diagram 8-45

The *rebounding* and *fast break responsibilities* are shown in the diagram for a typical situation that might occur. *(Diagram 8-46)*

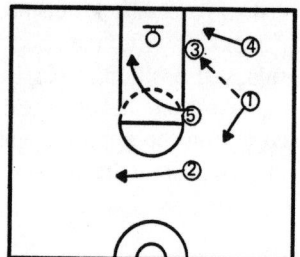

Diagram 8-46

Attack number 3

Man and Ball Movement	Outside Shooting	Tempo of Attackers	Low Post Action	Size
Considerable	Necessary	Rapid	Stressed	Normal

The motion begins with a pass from a guard (1) to a man from a low post position (4) breaking out to a wing spot. After the pass 1 starts down the lane, looping back to a wing position on the off-ball side. 3 cuts off his move to a low *post* position on the ball side looking for an advantage position on the defensive man in that area. 2 moves over to take a point position. *(Diagram 8-47)*

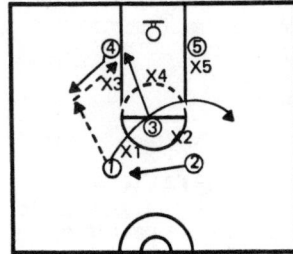

Diagram 8-47

If 4 cannot hit 3 at the low post, he passes out to 2 at the point. 2 passes to 1 at the wing and 4 goes to the *open spot* in the middle of the zone looking for a quick pass from 1 for a *good percentage shot*. *(Diagram 8-48)*

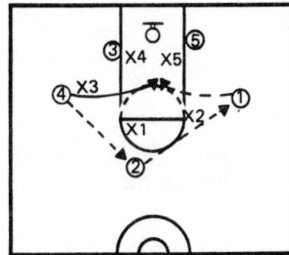

Diagram 8-48

If 4 does not receive a pass in the lane, he continues down toward the baseline under 5 and out to a spot behind 5's *screen* looking for a pass for a good percentage shot, or to dump the ball into 5 at the low *post* if the defense makes an adjustment to permit 4's shot. *(Diagram 8-49)*

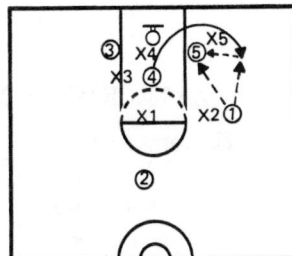

Diagram 8-49

If 1 cannot get the ball to either 4 or 5, he passes out to 2 at the point. 5 then moves across the lane and under 3's *screen* as 2 maneuvers to get him the ball for a quick shot. The pass may go directly to 3 if the defense adjusts to stop 5, leaving 3 in an advantage position at the low *post. (Diagram 8-50)*

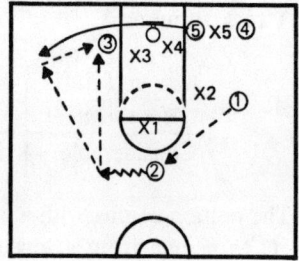

Diagram 8-50

ROTATION

If 2 cannot pass to either 3 or 5, he passes across to 1 who has returned to a guard spot. 4 and 5 shape up at the low post positions as 3 pops up to the high post. *(Diagram 8-51)*

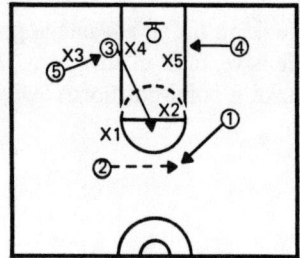

Diagram 8-51

As 1 receives the ball, 4 comes out to a wing position on the ball side and the motion is under way again. 1 cuts through and 3 rolls down to the low *post. (Diagram 8-52)*

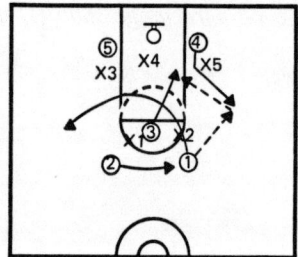

Diagram 8-52

ATTACKING A 2-3 ZONE FROM A 2-2-1 ALIGNMENT
Attack number 1

Man and Ball Movement	Outside Shooting	Tempo of Attackers	Low Post Action	Size
Limited	Necessary	Normal	Normal	Normal

One of the wings (4) should move to a high *post* position at the free-throw line. The guard (1) should not have much trouble getting the ball to him at this spot. This will force X4 to step out and cover him. The other guard (2) drops low to a *post* and 5 takes a low *post* position on the other side. *(Diagram 8-53)*

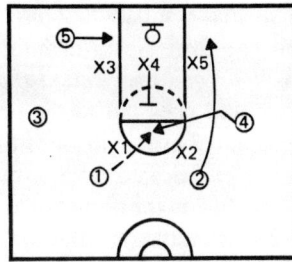

Diagram 8-53

4 looks inside to hit either 5 or 2 at their low posts or out at the wing to 3 if X3 has dropped back to successfully cover 5. *(Diagram 8-54)*

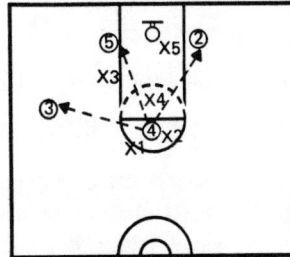

Diagram 8-54

If the ball goes to 3, X3 will be forced to jump out to cover him and X4 will drop down to cover 5. 4 can take a step or two to a mid-*post* spot looking for an immediate return pass and a quick shot from the *good percentage shooting area*. If X4 recovers and stops him, the ball can be flipped directly to 5 at the basket. *(Diagram 8-55)*

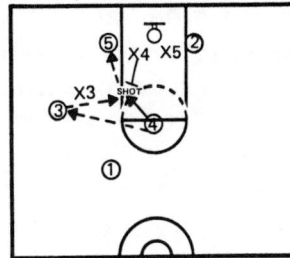

Diagram 8-55

VARIATION

In this variation, 2 will drop to the wing spot instead of going to the low post after the pass to 4. *(Diagram 8-56)*

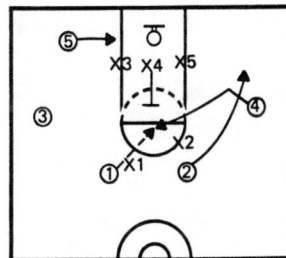

Diagram 8-56

This makes a pass to 2 easy because there is no one there to cover him, and so he may have a *good percentage shot*. 5 crosses the lane and goes out to the corner on the ball side and 3 drops down to fill the spot at the low *post* vacated by 5. Now 2 can pass directly to 5 in the corner or to 3 at the basket if X3 has moved in the wrong direction. 5 should be open in the corner for an easy shot, since X5 will have to come out to cover 2 at the wing. *(Diagram 8-57)*

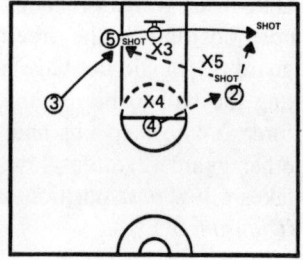

Diagram 8-57

ROTATION

In the orginal motion, if 3 does not hit anyone inside he can pass back out to 1 in the guard spot. 2 quickly moves out to the other guard spot. 5 crosses over into the corner away from the ball as 4 goes to the wing spot on the same side. *(Diagram 8-58)*

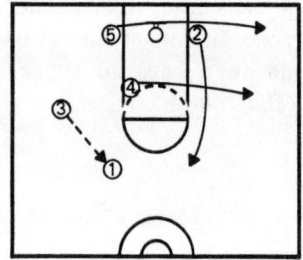

Diagram 8-58

Now 3 flashes to the high *post* for a pass from 2 and 1 drops down to the low *post* or to a wing spot on his side. Everything is the same as it was on the other side. 3 can hit 1 or 5. *(Diagram 8-59)*

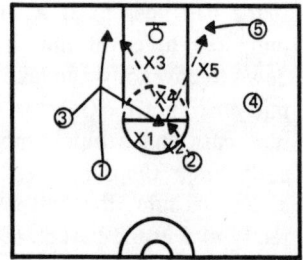

Diagram 8-59

If 3 passes out to 4 he should expect an immediate return pass for a quick shot as the defense adjusts. *(Diagram 8-60)*

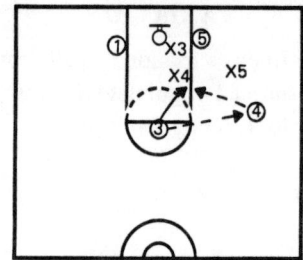

Diagram 8-60

ATTACKING A 2-3 ZONE FROM A 2-3 ALIGNMENT

Attack number 1

Man and Ball Movement	Outside Shooting	Tempo of Attackers	Low Post Action	Size
Considerable	Necessary	Rapid	Normal	Normal

2 begins the attack with a pass to 4. He then cuts down the lane and out into the corner on the ball side. 5 moves over to a high *post* position on the ball side. 1 fills 2's vacated spot and 3 angles down toward the basket on the off-ball side. *(Diagram 8-61)*

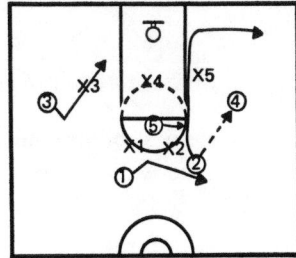

Diagram 8-61

As soon as 2 has gone through, 5 rolls to the basket expecting a pass from 4. 3 immediately comes across the lane and fills the *gap* at the mid-*post* area on the ball side. 4 may hit either 2, 3, or 5 if one of them is open in this *overloaded* situation. *(Diagram 8-62)*

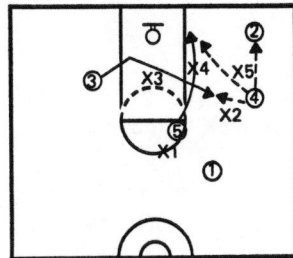

Diagram 8-62

ROTATION

If not, he passes back out front to 1. 1 dribbles it across to be in position to swing the ball to the other side. 3 goes to the wing position on that side, 5 comes to the high post and 2 returns to his original guard's position. *(Diagram 8-63)*

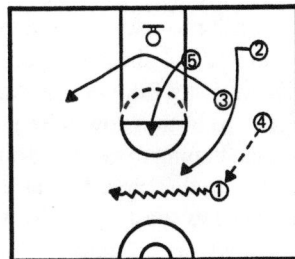

Diagram 8-63

Now the motion is run again as before. 1 passes to 3 and cuts down the lane and out into the corner on the ball side. 5 moves over to a high *post* position on the ball side. 2 fills 1's vacated spot and 4 angles down toward the basket on the off-ball side. *(Diagram 8-64)*

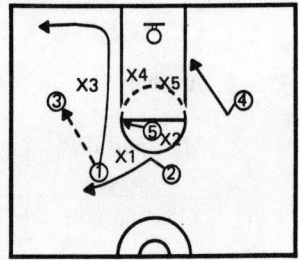

Diagram 8-64

The same possibilities now exist as was true on the other side. *(Diagram 8-65)*

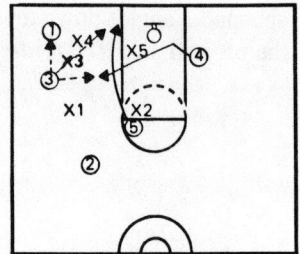

Diagram 8-65

Attack number 2

Man and Ball Movement	Outside Shooting	Tempo of Attackers	Low Post Action	Size
Normal	Necessary	Normal	Normal	Normal

The motion begins with an outside guard (1) passing to a wing (3) in the *gap* between X1 and X3. 1 then goes diagonally across the lane away from his pass and the middle man (4) rolls to a low *post* position on the ball side hoping to get an advantage position on a man in that area. 5 steps down to the off-ball side low post to be in position for the rebound, and 2 moves over to fill 1's spot. *(Diagram 8-66)*

Diagram 8-66

If 3 cannot get a shot or hit 4 at the low post, he passes back to 2 at the point. 2 then quickly passes to 1 who has ducked under 5's *screen* for a jump shot in the *good percentage shooting area*. *(Diagram 8-67)*

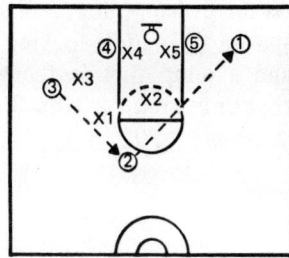

Diagram 8-67

If 1 cannot shoot or dump the ball into 5 at the low *post*, he dribbles out toward the point into the *gap* between X5 and X2. While this is happening, 2 cuts down the lane under 4 and out to an open spot on the weak side. 3 moves into the point spot to receive a pass from 1. As soon as he does, he quickly looks to hit 2 behind 4's screen for a good percentage shot or pass to 4 in an advantage position at the low *post*. *(Diagram 8-68)*

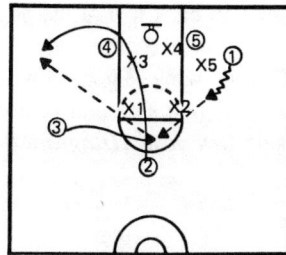

Diagram 8-68

Attack number 3

Man and Ball Movement	Outside Shooting	Tempo of Attackers	Low Post Action	Size
Considerable	Necessary	Rapid	Stressed	Normal

To begin this motion, the guard with the ball (2) dribbles into the *gap* between X1 and X2 in an attempt to commit X2 to him. As he does so, 1 steps behind him to receive a pass from 2. As soon as he receives the ball, he quickly moves it to 5 who is playing in the *seam* at the wing. This forces X5 to come up to cover 5 or he will have an open shot. 4 rolls to the low *post* in an attempt to get an advantage position on X4. *(Diagram 8-69)*

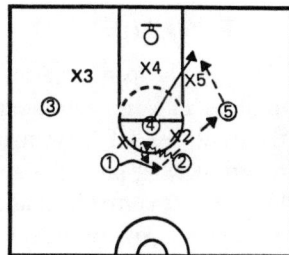

Diagram 8-69

As this is happening, 3 breaks into the open spot in the middle looking for a quick pass and a jump shot in the *good percentage shooting area*. 2 fills 3's vacated spot. *(Diagram 8-70)*

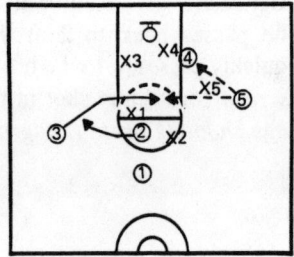

Diagram 8-70

If none of these passes are possible, 5 passes the ball back to 1 at the point and goes to the corner on the other side. 1 quickly passes to 2 at the wing. 3 goes down to the low post on the off-ball side and 4 moves to the strong-side low *post. (Diagram 8-71)*

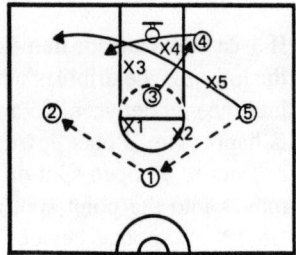

Diagram 8-71

Now 2 can hit 5 behind 4's screen or pass directly to 4 if he has an advantage position at the low *post. (Diagram 8-72)*

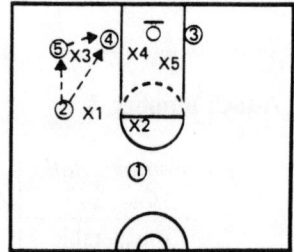

Diagram 8-72

ROTATION

If nothing is open, 2 passes back to 1. 1 now dribbles into the gap attempting to commit the front two defensive men to him. 5 and 3 return to wing positions and 4 moves to the high post. 2 comes behind 1 to be in position to receive a pass from him. *(Diagram 8-73)*

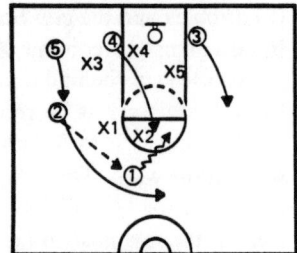

Diagram 8-73

As before, 1 flips 2 the ball. 2 passes back to 5. 4 rolls to the low *post* and 3 flashes into the middle. *(Diagram 8-74)*

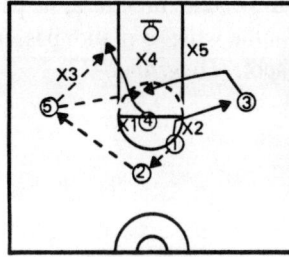

Diagram 8-74

Attack number 4

Man and Ball Movement	Outside Shooting	Tempo of Attackers	Low Post Action	Size
Considerable	Necessary	Rapid	Normal	Normal

A guard (1) begins by passing to a wing (3). As the pass is made, 5 rolls to the strongside low *post* attempting to get advantage position and a pass. The offside wing (4) flashes into the middle looking for a pass and a jump shot in the *good percentage shooting area*. 2 drops down to fill 4's vacated spot. *(Diagram 8-75)*

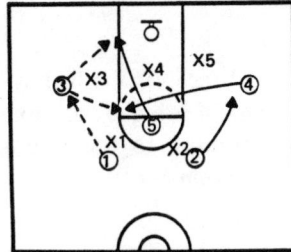

Diagram 8-75

If 4 does not receive a pass at the low post, he moves out to the corner. If he receives the pass from 3, 4 rolls to the basket hoping for a pass. If he does not get the ball, he continues out to the wing on the weak side. 2 comes to the open spot in the middle expecting a pass from 5. *(Diagram 8-76)*

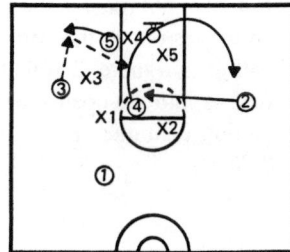

Diagram 8-76

If 5 cannot hit 4 or 2, he passes back out to 3
at the wing. 3 in turn passes to 1 at the guard
spot. *(Diagram 8-77)*

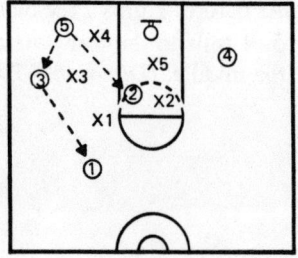

Diagram 8-77

ROTATION

1 quickly moves the ball over to be in position to pass to 2 at the other wing. 2 and 4
have exchanged positions as 5 passes out of
the corner to 3. 5 steps into the low post on
the off-ball side. *(Diagram 8-78)*

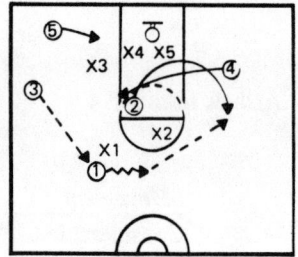

Diagram 8-78

As 2 receives the ball at the wing, 4 and 5
cross, 4 going to the strongside low *post* and
5 coming to the strongside high *post*.
(Diagram 8-79)

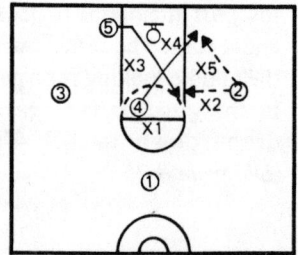

Diagram 8-79

If 4 does not receive the ball at the low post,
he moves out to the corner. After 2 gets the
ball to him there, 5 rolls to the basket and 3
flashes into the open spot in the middle. The
motion continues in this manner. *(Diagram
8-80)*

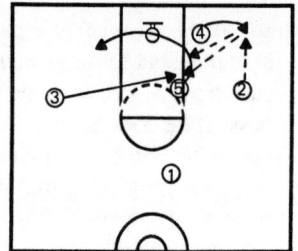

Diagram 8-80

Chapter 9

ATTACKING THE UNORTHODOX ZONE DEFENSES

To begin, a definition and an identification of the various unorthodox zone defenses should be offered:

Combination: Playing some men man-to-man and some zone. There are three major types—the box-and-one, diamond-and-one, and the triangle and two.

Multiple: This defines the practice of alternating defenses—changing from one defense to another in a variety of situations.

Match Up: A defense that rotates into an alignment that corresponds to its opponent's alignment or style of attack, sometimes using zone principles, sometimes using man-to-man tactics.

More and more teams today are going to some form of unorthodox defensive strategy to counter the ever-improving offensive skills. You need to prepare your team to meet these defenses, at least psychologically. Merely understanding what the defense is attempting to do is sometimes sufficient to avoid total confusion. Coupled with techniques of man-to-man play, precise application of the principles already advocated would provide a team with adequate weapons to combat any of the unorthodox defenses.

Let's deal with each type in more detail:

COMBINATION

A. Box-and-One (Diagram 9-1)

Four men play in a zone defense while one man plays man-to-man. This is usually done to neutralize one outstanding player, but on occasion the one man is allowed to move freely and aggressively after the ball. The object of the box usually is to force the outside shot while containing the individual star. It also attempts to prevent close-in shots. This is a weak defense against good shooters and it is susceptible to penetration at the gaps.

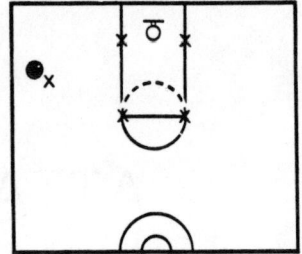

Diagram 9-1

The best approach to attacking this defense is to set one man at the point in the gap between the defensive guards. He should make an effort to penetrate this seam and draw the two men to him, giving more room to his wing men. Now the motion needs to vary only slightly from any attack used against an even man front zone. The variation, of course, is to be seen in the use of the individual being pressured in a 1-on-1 basis. He must be content to remain outside or near the baseline most of the time. He can crash the boards after shots and move inside to an off-side low post when the ball has gone inside low, but basically he must be content to serve as a decoy. This, in itself, is very valuable as the defense must be constantly aware of his position and movement on the court. This defensive preoccupation will help to open up other offensive possibilities.

Two motions are offered here for your consideration and to illustrate some of the many possibilities:

Attack number 1

1 attempts to penetrate the seam, hopefully drawing X2 to him. He will then pass to 3 who may have an uncontested shot sitting in the *gap* as he is. The man drawing single coverage moves out to the opposite corner. *(Diagram 9-2)*

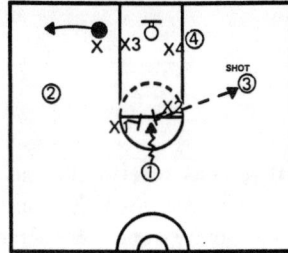

Diagram 9-2

3 can dribble down toward the baseline, forcing X4 to come out on him. This may permit a pass inside to 4 at the low *post* if he has advantage position on X3 coming across to help out. 1 and 2 rotate over and ● comes in to get offside *rebounding* position. *(Diagram 9-3)*

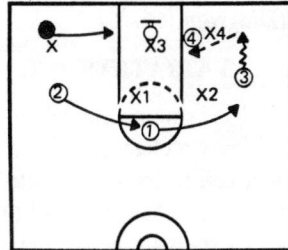

Diagram 9-3

If nothing is open, 3 passes back out to 1. As this pass is made, 4 comes across the lane, goes under ●'s *screen* and out to a wing position looking for a pass from 2. *(Diagram 9-4)*

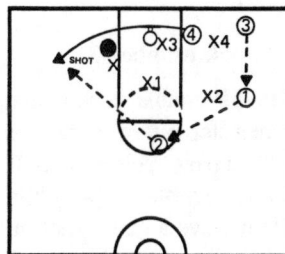

Diagram 9-4

After 1's pass to 2 he head-hunts down for X4. 3 comes in toward the basket and steps out behind 1's *screen* looking for a pass from 2 and a shot in the *good percentage shooting area*. *(Diagram 9-5)*

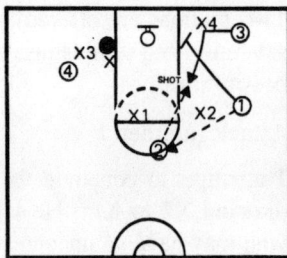

Diagram 9-5

If 4 does receive the pass from 2, ● will *screen* away for 1. X3 must come out to stop the shot by 4 and if ●'s screen can prevent X4 from coming across to help out, 1 should have a layup at the basket. 3 can step into the middle if it is open or he can move back out to the wing. ● continues to the corner and now everything is the same as before and the motion can begin again on this side. *(Diagram 9-6)*

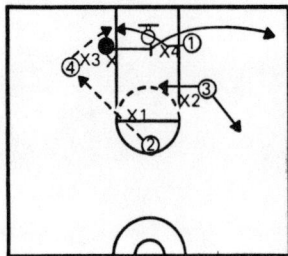

Diagram 9-6

VARIATION

As 1 is bringing the ball up, 3 can *screen* X2, giving 1 a chance to dribble by and down. 3 will roll to the basket after his screen and 4 will step out to force X4 to make a decision. If X4 stays inside, 4 may have a shot. If he does not, 3 may get a return pass for a layup. If X3 comes across to help out, 2 can drop down to the vacated spot, looking for a pass at the basket. Of course, 1 may shoot after the screen if no one picks him up. *(Diagram 9-7)*

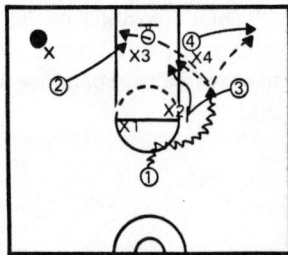

Diagram 9-7

Attack number 2

In this double stack alignment, both baseline men step out behind *screens* by the top men. 1 can pass to either side. If he passes to 4, X4 will have the responsibility for both men. 4 may have a quick shot or he may be able to dump the ball inside to 3 at the low *post*. *(Diagram 9-8)*

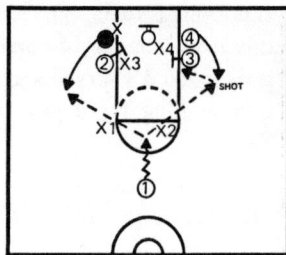

Diagram 9-8

If the ball goes to ●, 2 will step out to the corner to receive a pass from ●. This will draw X3 out or 2 will have a shot. ● cuts through to the basket after his pass and then *screens* across the lane for 3. If X4 is scraped off on the screen, 3 will have a shot at the basket. 1 fills ●'s vacated spot and ● takes offside *rebounding* position. *(Diagram 9-9)*

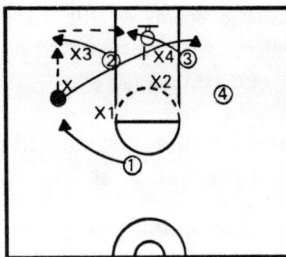

Diagram 9-9

2 passes out to 1 at the wing and then *screens* for 3 to step out behind for a shot. As 1 starts his dribble across, ● sets a blind *screen* on X2 and 4 drops down looking for a pass at the basket. *(Diagram 9-10)*

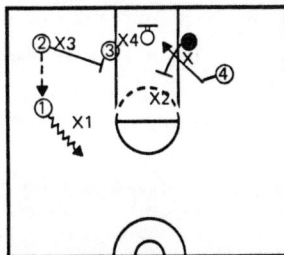

Diagram 9-10

1 has two pass possibilities. The men are also reset and the motion may begin again. *(Diagram 9-11)*

Diagram 9-11

B. Diamond-and-One (Diagram 9-12)

The diamond-and-one is identical in intent to the box-and-one. The difference is to be seen in the alignment. It presents an odd-man front, forcing a team to adjust its attack somewhat. This defense is also weak against good outside shooting, and it is vulnerable to a strong attack at the baseline and at the pivot. Once again, penetration by the offense

Diagram 9-12

at the seams of the zone is good strategy along with an overload principle to open up good percentage shots.

Two motions are offered as suggestions for constructing an attack:

Attack number 1

1 passes to 2 away from the side of individual coverage. 2 then dribbles at X3 forcing coverage by him. As this happens, 4 steps out from his low post position and 3 rolls down to fill that vacated spot. *(Diagram 9-13)*

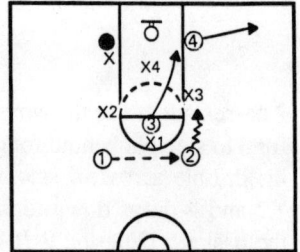

Diagram 9-13

Now X4 must cover 4 at the side or he will have a shot. With 3 at the low *post*, the defense must make an immediate adjustment or 3 will have a shot at the basket. *(Diagram 9-14)*

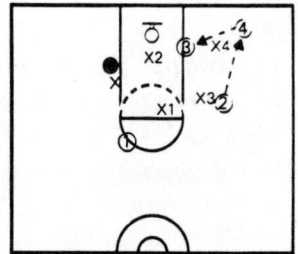

Diagram 9-14

If this is not open, 4 passes back out to 2 and ● sets a blind *screen* for 1 to use going to the basket. If he is not covered, 2 may lob it to him or pass directly to 3 if X2 steps over to cover. *(Diagram 9-15)*

Diagram 9-15

● provides a pick for 2 who dribbles to the point. As this is happening, 3 comes out to the wing and 4 goes to the low *post*. 1 immediately returns to a guard spot outside. ● drops down to be in position for an off-side *rebound*. (*Diagram 9-16*)

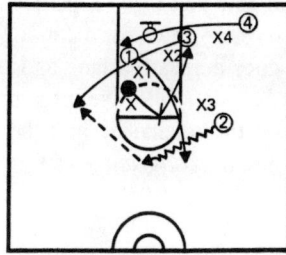

Diagram 9-16

After 3 receives the pass from 2, he can dribble to the baseline and take the shot or dump the ball into 4 at the low *post* if he has advantage position. Again, the alignment is the same and the motion continues on this side. (*Diagram 9-17*)

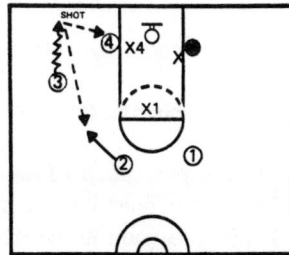

Diagram 9-17

Attack number 2

2 passes to 1 away from 0's side. 1 now dribbles at X2. As this is happening, 4 comes across the lane, under 3's *screen* and out to the deep wing spot looking for a pass and a shot in the *good percentage shooting area*. If X4 fights through, 4 may dump the ball into 3 at the low *post* if he has advantage position. 1 cuts through the lane and 2 fills his vacated spot. (*Diagram 9-18*)

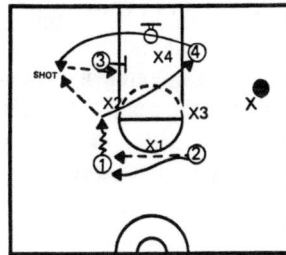

Diagram 9-18

4 passes back out to 2 and steps into the low post. 2 passes to 1 stepping out to the guard spot. ● *screens* down for 3 coming under and out to the deep wing. 1 tries to get him the ball for a quick jump shot. (*Diagram 9-19*)

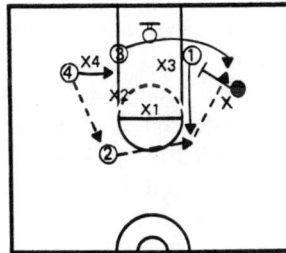

Diagram 9-19

If this can't go, 3 passes back out to 1 and *screens* down for 4 coming across the lane. ● goes across the lane and out to the wing on the other side. Now the offense is realigned on the other side and the motion can begin again. *(Diagram 9-20)*

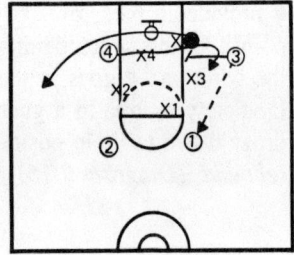

Diagram 9-20

C. Triangle-and-two (Diagram 9-21)

In this defense, the three deep men use a triangle zone defense while the front two players pick up man-to-man. The purpose here is to pressure the outside men while holding to good inside rebounding position. The two outside men can use a variety of tactics such as double-teaming, switching, and jamming of the passing lanes. It may be confusing to teams initially if they forget to move ball and men. It is weak against good outside shooting and is vulnerable to penetration at the seams. The offensive guards must be very active to keep the defensive guards occupied and away from the action inside.

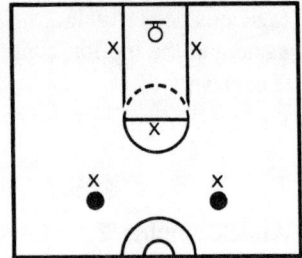

Diagram 9-21

Attack number 1

To keep the two defensive guards busy, 1 crosses in front of 2's dribble and goes to the wing (if his man does not go with him, 1 should hook back to an open spot for a pass outside from 2). 4 steps out for a pass from 2 and then dribbles a step or two toward the middle. 3 rolls to the low post and 5 crosses the lane to a deep wing spot. 4 may have a shot if X1 goes with 3. *(Diagram 9-22)*

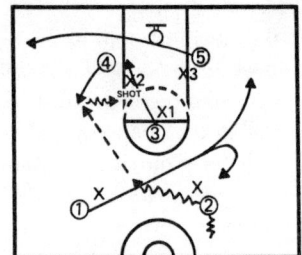

Diagram 9-22

4 may pass to 5 for a shot if X2 does not come out on him, or either 4 or 5 may dump directly inside to 3 at the low *post* if he has advantage position. 1 and 2 exchange positions. *(Diagram 9-23)*

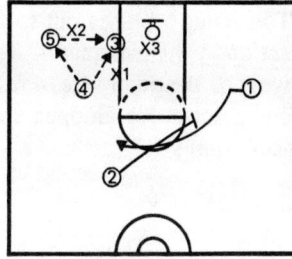

Diagram 9-23

ROTATION

4 passes back out to 1 and goes to the low post on the other side as 3 goes to the wing on the same side. 5 moves all the way over to the same position on the other side. 1 dribbles over to the other guard spot and 2 sets up at the short 17 position. *(Diagram 9-24)*

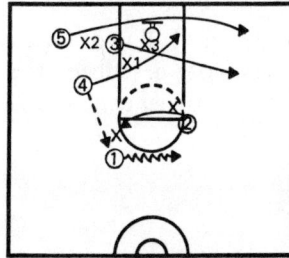

Diagram 9-24

If the zone has shifted to cover the three inside men, 1 and 2 might work a little dovetail action from the short 17. *(Diagram 9-25)*

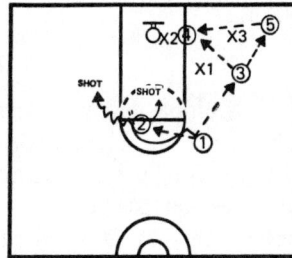

Diagram 9-25

Attack number 2

2 screens for 1 to come behind to pass to 5. After receiving the pass, 5 dribbles toward the baseline. 3 rolls to the low *post* forcing coverage by either X2 or X1 going with him. 4 watches this defensive reaction and then goes away from the coverage. X3 is forced to step out to cover 5 or 5 will have a short shot *(Diagram 9-26)*

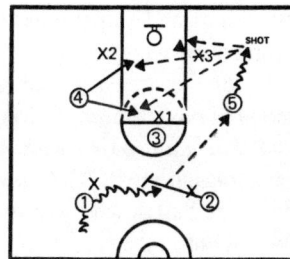

Diagram 9-26

To rotate, 5 passes out to 2 after a crossing action by the two guards. 3 moves over to the wing on the other side, 4 rolls to the low post and 5 looks for an open spot in the middle. *(Diagram 9-27)*

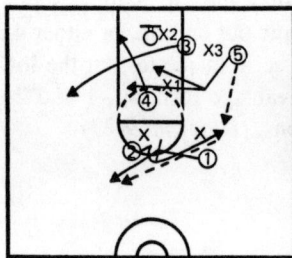

Diagram 9-27

1 gets the ball to 3 who repeats the action as previously described. The motion continues in this manner until a shot is taken. *(Diagram 9-28)*

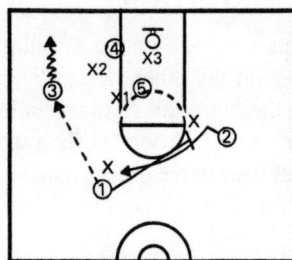

Diagram 9-28

MULTIPLE DEFENSES

Multiple defenses can be terribly upsetting if a team does not possess the ability to change pattern on signal, or if it has a limited variety of methods of attack. Usually a team employing multiple defenses will keep all five men in the same defense but change them periodically. For example, after a field goal a team may be in a full court man-to-man press. After a missed field goal attempt it will be in a short zone defense. A free-throw keys a mid-court press. A turnover signals a change of zone type, and so on. Each time its opponent comes down court it is faced with the challenge of identifying the defense it is attacking, and sometimes the defense is disguised to create an even greater problem of recognition.

Presses are easily identifiable, causing little concern to a team, at least in terms of recognition. As long as each individual has one man confronting him *and that man moves with him as he goes downcourt*, the team is facing a man-to-man press. The players merely empty downcourt and let the dribbler bring the ball down by himself. If movement by the offense does not produce movement in the same direction by the defense, some form of zone press is in evidence. This is why it is important that after gaining possession of the ball a team always set up in the same manner to break a zone press. Adjustment from this alignment is easy, but adjustment against zone tactics without *team* organization is not so easy.

In the front court the offense may not be so easily able to determine what they are facing. Sending a guard through is a time-honored technique of distinguishing defensive reactions. What is required, of course, is an alignment from which a team can run both a man-to-man motion *and* zone motion. Then, all that is required is some form of key to identify the type of defense (a verbal call, a visual signal, etc.) to enable a team to react and initiate the proper action. It is suggested that a coach find a zone attack that closely corresponds to his man-to-man system in terms of alignment so that an easy and quick adjustment can be made.

Match Up

The match-up defense is a true test of a team's composure, its concept of offensive fundamentals, and the kind of job done by the coach in practice. Compared to multiple defenses, the problem when facing a match-up does not appear to be nearly as imposing initially. The offensive team is usually permitted to take whatever positions it chooses on the court without having to worry about recognizing defensive alignments—but then the trouble begins!

Simply stated, a match-up is a means by which defensive personnel are placed in corresponding floor positions to that of the offense to give it the option of utilizing man-to-man or zone principles of attack. The idea is to confuse the opponents—to appear to be in a zone defense when they are running their man-to-man attack, and to appear to be in a man-to-man defense when they are running their zone defense. It hopes to reduce the effectiveness of offensive maneuvers (screens, cuts, posting, etc.) by keeping pressure on the ball while contesting leads, two-timing, trapping, stunting, and jamming passing lanes. A tall order? You bet it is! Yet teams succumb to its tactics if they allow themselves to be intimidated and are not well prepared.

How do we prepare? Let's begin with a few simple principles:

1. *Movement* is of major importance! The match-up has the same weaknesses as do all other defenses (*more* really), but it hides these weaknesses quite well because the defense does not always react to offensive movement but rather *dictates* to it. Movement creates defensive problems. One can never forget that! Keeping players very active and alert is essential. If the players simply stand around when they become confused, they have fallen into the trap and the match-up has won.

2. *Vary the points of attack quickly.* This is another part of the movement principle Many offensive teams rely only on perimeter passing and posting because the defense resembles a zone. This is a mistake. Man-to-man principles *and* zone principles must be combined to give a team the ability to probe in a variety of ways and in a variety of places.

3. *Cut through the defense.* Part of the assignment for the defense is to pick up cutters or trade men as they move from area to area. This becomes particularly hard when a man is run diagonally through the defense or when he cuts through from the blind baseline side.

Rather than make it more complicated than necessary for the players, perhaps the best rule to follow is to stick to your basic man-to-man continuity and simply add other options that are zone oriented. With enough practice, a team can be conditioned to react to problems as they are encountered if they truly understand all the objectives their offense is trying to accomplish.

The following patterns are offered to provide some examples of how the two principles of attack can be combined:

Attack number 1

The guard on the weak side (1) passes to the wing on his side (3) and cuts through to the corner. Following close after his cut is 2 who stops at the strongside low post. 5 flashes to the high post right after 2's cut. This gives 3 three quick pass opportunities. 4 fills 2's vacated spot. *(Diagram 9-29)*

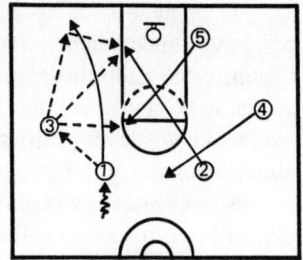

Diagram 9-29

If 3 can't hit any of these players, he passes out to 4 and runs a shuffle cut off 5 at the high post. As 4 is attempting to pass to 3 on the way to the bucket, 1 is coming out to a guard spot and 2 is moving out to a deep wing. *(Diagram 9-30)*

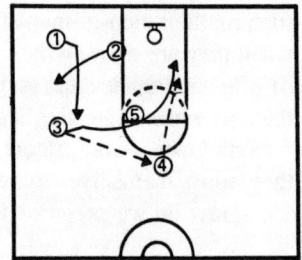

Diagram 9-30

Now the ball is moved across to 1 and then down to 2 at the deep wing. After his pass 4 makes a cut to the basket around 5 at the high post. 1 goes diagonally down to the baseline on the off-ball side. 2 may hit the cutting 4 or pass the ball to 5 at the side post if he is open. *(Diagram 9-31)*

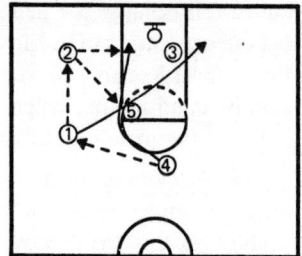

Diagram 9-31

After making the cut, 4 continues across the lane to set a screen for 3 coming to the ball. After 4's cut, 5 steps out to the guard spot to receive a pass from 2. 1 comes out to the guard spot on the other side to take a swing pass from 5. *(Diagram 9-32)*

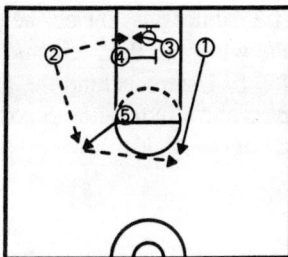

Diagram 9-32

ROTATION

With 4 moving out to the wing spot, the team is now ready to run the same motion to the other side. 1 hits 4 and cuts to the corner, followed closely by 5 on his way to the basket. 3 pops up to the high post behind the cut. The motion continues until a shot is taken. *(Diagram 9-33)*

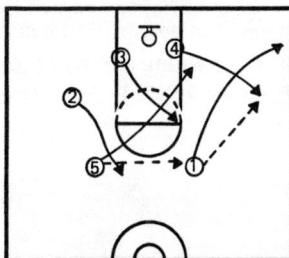

Diagram 9-33

Attack number 2

From a 1-3-1 alignment 1 passes to the strongside wing (3). 3 then passes to 2 who has cut through to the baseline and out behind 5's screen. 3 cuts through to the weakside low post after his pass. 2 may have a shot behind the screen if the defense has not adjusted. *(Diagram 9-34)*

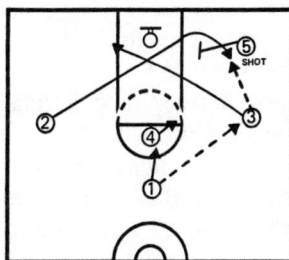

Diagram 9-34

1 now follows 3, cutting to the basket and using 5's screen. 5 immediately steps up toward the high post providing a screen for 1 after he has screened for 2. 4 has moved out to fill 3's vacated wing spot. *(Diagram 9-35)*

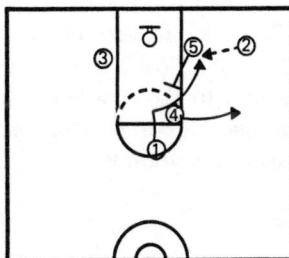

Diagram 9-35

If 2 cannot pass inside, he passes out to 4 at the wing and then screens toward the basket for 1. 1 steps behind the pick looking for a pass and a jump shot. 5 pops up to the point. *(Diagram 9-36)*

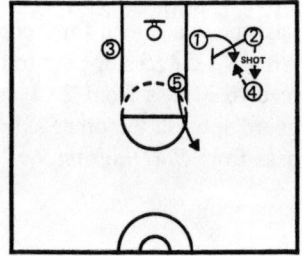

Diagram 9-36

After 2 screens for 1 he continues across the lane providing a moving screen for 3 coming from the off-ball side. *(Diagram 9-37)*

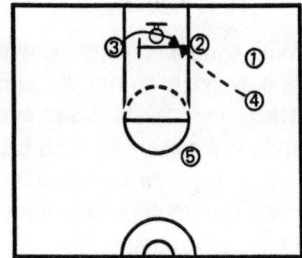

Diagram 9-37

If 4 can't get the ball to either 1 or 3 inside, he passes to 5 at the point. 2 now pops up to the short 17, and 5 either runs a dovetail action with him after a pass or he dribbles around his high post screen on the way to the basket. 4 fills the point and 1 comes out to the wing. *(Diagram 9-38)*

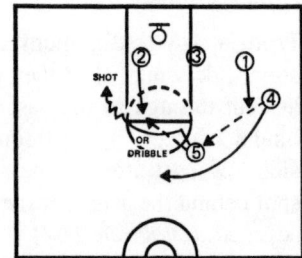

Diagram 9-38

To rotate, 2 passes out to 4. 4 then passes to 5 hooking back to the wing spot. 3 comes across to the low post and 1 cuts through behind 3's post looking for a pass and a jump shot. *(Diagram 9-39)*

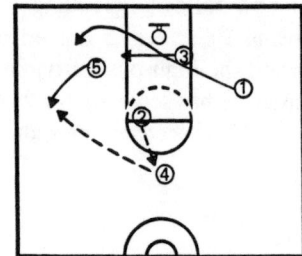

Diagram 9-39

Attack number 3

In this 1-4 set, it becomes difficult for the defense to do anything but take each player man-to-man. The defense at least must honor each of the four high men or they will have a quick uncontested shot after receiving a pass. The ball may go to a wing on either side. In this case it has gone to 5. 4 will now roll to the basket looking for a pass and a layup. 3 steps across to fill his vacated spot as 2 sprints through to the strongside corner. Any one of these three men may be open for a quick jump shot if the defense has misplayed them. *(Diagram 9-40)*

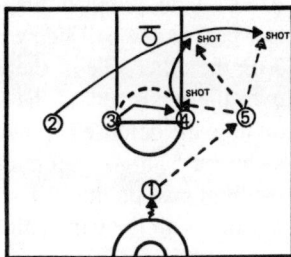

Diagram 9-40

A pass could go to a post (4). It does not change the action of the men on the off-ball side. 5 quickly dives to the basket after the pass to 4 looking for a blind pig. If 4 can't hit him, he will dribble out to the wing. The options are now identical to the ones previously described. *(Diagram 9-41)*

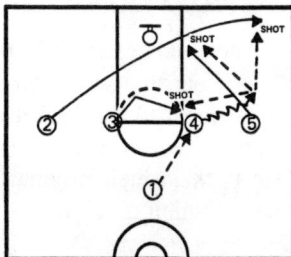

Diagram 9-41

From here the defense is forced to stay with men and the scramble attack is run. 5 passes back out to the point and cuts through and out to a wing. 3 rolls to a low post and 2 screens down for 4. *(Diagram 9-42)*

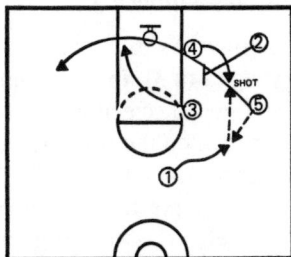

Diagram 9-42

1 can hit 4 behind 2's screen or he can pass to 5 at the other wing. *(Diagram 9-43)*

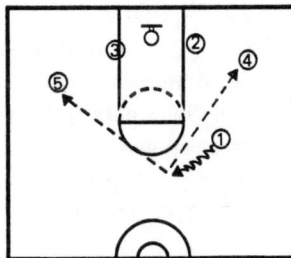

Diagram 9-43

After a wing pass (in this instance to 4), the low post on the ball side will screen away for 3 on the other side of the lane. 3 may come over the top or under the screen, depending on how the defense is playing him. 1 screens away for 5. 5 goes around the screen and to the high post on the ball side. 1 rolls back to balance with the ball again. *(Diagram 9-44)*

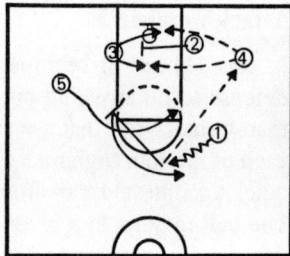

Diagram 9-44

ROTATION

If 3 does not get a pass he returns, goes under 2, and out to a wing. 4 passes back to 1. 5 goes down to the basket and then out to a wing under 4's crack-down block. The men are back in their original positions and the same motion is run again. *(Diagram 9-45)*

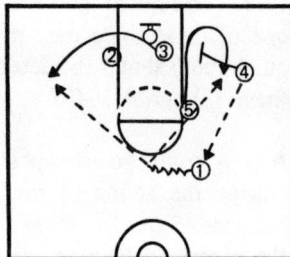

Diagram 9-45

Attack number 4

1 brings the ball upcourt and passes to either wing (2 or 3). In this example he passes to 3 and uses a screen by 2 to attempt to rub off his man on the way to the basket. After the pass to 3, 4 comes under 5 (clearing out his low post position and opening it up for 1 if the defense is covering men and not zones) and out to a deep wing position looking for a pass from 3. *(Diagram 9-46)*

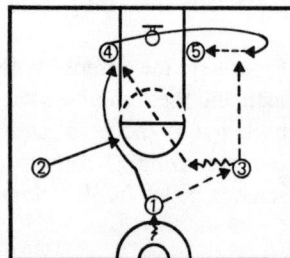

Diagram 9-46

If 3 doesn't hit 4 or 1, he passes across to 2 after 2 clears himself for a pass. After this pass, 5 comes under 1's low post position looking for a pass at the deep wing position. 3 screens down, meeting 4 at the box so that 4 can step out to a position near the short 17 looking for a pass and a jump shot. *(Diagram 9-47)*

Diagram 9-47

The motion continues in this manner until a shot is taken. Basically, the offense is looking for a shot in the good percentage shooting area or to get the ball inside to the low post on the strong side if that man is in an advantage position. This action would be quite effective against changing defenses as it employs maneuvers that are effective against both zone and man principles. *(Diagram 9-48)*

Diagram 9-48

Chapter 10

ORGANIZING THE OVERALL ATTACK AGAINST THE EXTENDED ZONES

The approaches to breaking an extended zone press are many, but a few simple principles are basic to any design and should, therefore, be given some attention here:

1. DEVELOP AND MAINTAIN POISE

The success of any press depends to a very large extent on the attitude of the opponent. Many teams simply beat themselves when they encounter full court pressure. Credit must, of course, be given the hustle, determination, and execution of many teams employing the press, but more often than not, it's bad passing, the inability of a player to see the open man, missed assignments, confusion, etc. that are the result of a lack of poise.

When any team spreads itself over an entire court, no matter how quick and intelligent it is, holes open up, seams become wider, and areas of defensive coverage become larger. In theory, at least, this *should* be a weak defense—and it is *if* a team can avoid the panic that leads to mistakes. Very easy to *say*—not so easy to do! Daily work against extended defenses is a necessity in the game of basketball today. It does very little good to merely *talk* to a team about remaining poised. Situations can be devised to simulate the conditions in a game that produce panic. Double-teaming, trapping, jump switching—all sorts of strategic methods of play are possible in drill situations. Admittedly, playing against the enemy under game conditions is considerably more disconcerting than playing against the friendly face of a teammate in practice, but a lot can be learned from seeing and feeling the reactions of others, especially when the coach makes it highly competitive.

2. ALWAYS EXPECT THE PRESS

If a team can be conditioned to react as though they were going to be pressed *each* time the opponent scores, the element of surprise would not be a factor. Instinctively, players should head toward their assigned spots and be prepared mentally and physically to contend with anything. Seeing that an opponent is organized and confident is enough to discourage a lot of teams from pressing with the same degree of abandon that they might display against a disorganized and frightened team. Be ready!

3. BE AN INTELLIGENT INBOUNDER

The person inbounding the ball must have the capacity to read the situation facing his team in a split second. It may be that he will have to hustle after the ball and inbound quickly, or he may have to take as much time as possible to see to it that all his teammates are in position. In this instance, he should not pick up the ball until required or, if it is loose, he should wait for the official to retrieve it for him. Whatever the case, at no time should he pick up the ball with his back to the court, or more precisely, make any move until he's had a chance to survey the situation.

Most of the time he should have more than one man to whom he can inbound. In practice, he will learn to recognize certain keys that will help determine his choice. He must not become stereotyped—inbounding to his right each time, for example, could get him in trouble. Always making the same kind of pass, never threatening deep, or always picking out a favorite man are other stereotypic reactions that serve to illustrate this point.

4. BEAT THE PRESS BEFORE IT SETS UP

A press *does* take some time to form. It's well worth the effort and the time spent in practice drilling players to fulfill their responsibilities in the shortest possible time because nothing can be more devastating to a press than to have the other team get the ball inbounds and up court with a numbers advantage before the pressing team can really react. Hustle!

5. USE THE BASELINE

The inbounder needs to learn to make full use of the baseline. If he becomes planted in one spot, it greatly restricts the offensive team's mobility and gives the defense the opportunity to sit back and react to the passes.

6. DON'T GIVE GROUND TO PRESSURE

One of the biggest mistakes that a team can make is to allow pressure to intimidate it. A player without the ball *can't* give ground when he is being crowded or he will be run off the court. He must go at it, make contact, and release himself from it when it is to his advantage. This is a fundamental rule not to be violated!

7. TAKE INTELLIGENT COURT POSITION

The men on the court who are attempting to free themselves for an inbounds pass must not allow themselves to be forced too close to the sidelines or baseline. They should start their move more toward the middle of the court and far enough away from the baseline to have maneuverability. From here, they are in a relatively uncommitted position, and it becomes more difficult for the defense to determine what path they will take.

8. USE THE FAKE

Each man handling the ball or freeing himself for a pass has a weapon at his disposal that is particularly effective against zone presses—the fake. The extended zone defense is responsive to many things done in the offense: movement, feet position, direction of the dribble, alignment on the court, etc. A team can gain an advantage if it can disguise any of the keys used by the defense to direct its reactions. The fake pass is probably the most effective of all those available and should be used to good advantage.

9. MEET THE PASS

A team is truly flirting with disaster if its players stand and wait for the pass. This rule is as old as the game, and it is particularly important when combating extended defenses.

10. PROTECT THE BALL

If a player receives the pass with his back to the basket, he should pull the ball in close to his body to protect it, turn his head to get a good look at both his opponents and his teammates before pivoting and beginning a move up court. If he turns and makes a move before doing this, he endangers the ball, puts himself in jeopardy of being irretrievably trapped, and risks the charging foul.

11. SPREAD THE DEFENSE

Again, the full court is a large area for the defense to cover, and the offense makes it easier for them if it does not stay spread. A worthy goal to shoot for in the offensive alignment and pattern is to have a teammate available for a pass in front of the ball handler and to his left and right at all times. To illustrate:

(Diagram 10-1)

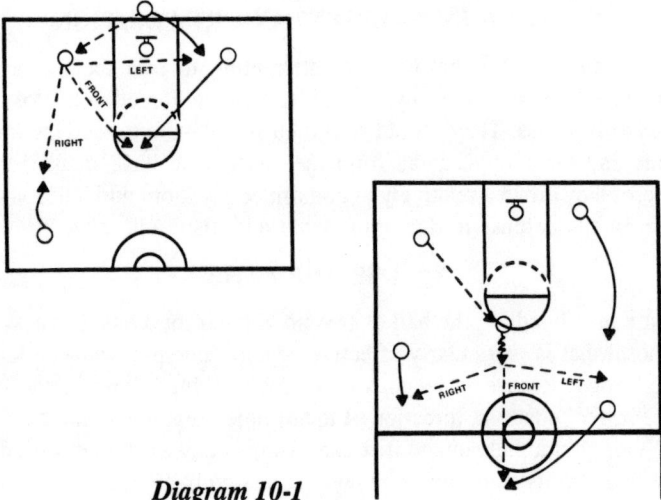

Diagram 10-1

It may not be possible to always achieve this, but a team should at least try to have a man to the ball handler's left and right.

Now the most critical aspect of this principle: the *correct distance between players must be maintained at all times*. If the ball is *advanced*, the players should move down court to keep the spacing the same. If the ball handler *retreats*, his teammates have to move back toward the ball to continue to be available for a pass. About the worst thing that happens against the press is that the ball handler's teammates abandon him, moving downcourt and out of range of a pass. By the same token, they cannot stay too close, jamming the driving lanes and making it possible for one defensive man to cover more than one opponent at a time. *(Diagram 10-2)*

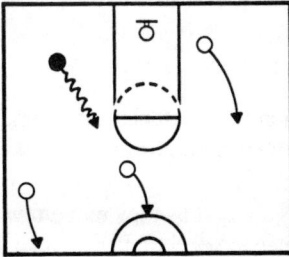

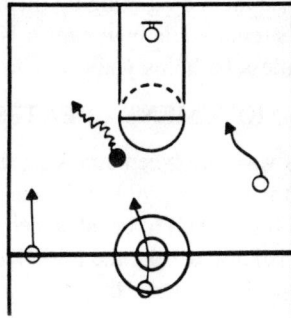

Diagram 10-2

12. GO AWAY FROM YOUR PASS

To follow one's pass is to violate the principle just advocated. This would bring two offensive players close together enabling *one* defensive man to influence the actions of both.

13. DRAW THE DOUBLE TEAM

An important offensive objective is to draw two men to the ball when facing a zone press. This will produce an open man somewhere on the court. The ball handler needs to keep his dribble and advance the ball as long as he is facing only one opponent. The instant a second opponent commits himself to the ball, that is when the pass should be made. This is a very hard lesson to teach. Because of a fear of getting trapped, players want to give up the ball too quickly. *The defensive team must be made to commit itself* so the offense can react. To do it otherwise is a risky business. From baseline to baseline the offensive team is looking for a numbers advantage, and this is the quickest way to produce it. When a man is being pressured after stopping his dribble, he must not turn his back or lose vision of the open areas of the court. Each man needs to work to develop the ability to step back with the dribble to give himself some room and to improve his perspective while still facing the pressure head on. With practice, players can be taught to look at *defensive* movements. It's not necessary to watch teammates since the ball handler is already familiar with their positions and adjustments. He does need to know what the defense is going to do, however. Their actions will dictate his reactions.

14.   GIVE THE PASSER A TARGET

Since the ball handler's focus of attention is on defensive movements, he may not always get a clear picture of the offensive adjustments. It is important, therefore, that his teammates indicate to him that they are open and help him to see them by getting up their hands as a target as they move toward the ball. It's remarkable how hard it is sometimes to *see* a player on a basketball court unless he helps you.

15.   MOVEMENT CREATES PROBLEMS FOR THE DEFENSE

As was true when attacking the short zones, movement of ball and men creates the biggest problem for the defense. Offensive personnel cannot stand, waiting for the ball to be advanced because they become sitting ducks, allowing the defense to take the initiative, get a clear picture of the passing angles, and spring traps when they choose.

16.   BEAT THE ZONE PRESS WITH PASSING

The dribble is the most effective weapon against a man-to-man press, but, because *areas* are being covered in the zone press, the dribble does little more than get a team in trouble. Of course this does not include the situation where a man has taken a pass in the middle, pivoted and found no defensive man covering him. Here, he can advance the ball on a dribble and produce a numbers advantage before the defense can react. But to try to dribble when a trap is imminent (unless busting the seam of the trap as a last resort) does not make sense. If a player can draw the double team to him, as previously described, quick accurate passes will cut the press to pieces.

17.   AVOID THE CORNERS AND SIDELINES

Teams trap in corners and near sidelines. They should be avoided if at all possible. If a ball is to be moved into these areas, it must be done with caution and the player handling the ball must have a clear picture of an escape route for the ball.

18.   DISREGARD PATTERNS WHEN A TEAMMATE
IS IN TROUBLE

Even with careful organization and precise execution, there will be several times during a game when things won't go quite as planned, and an individual will find himself in trouble. It's important that a team be flexible enough to adjust to the crisis and do what's necessary. Players must not be tied to a pattern to the degree that it robs them of their initiative and their imagination.

19.   CONTINUE TO PENETRATE AFTER CROSSING
THE MID-COURT LINE

Many teams make the mistake of crossing mid-court, heaving a sigh of relief, and setting up in another style of attack. If a team is really *attacking* the press, often this is the point when the defense is most vulnerable. Once the ball is by the front line of defense, a numbers advantage for the offense may exist. With the ball in the middle and sideline break lanes filled, a team may have exactly what they work so hard to achieve in their front court patterned attack.

20.   SIMPLICITY IS A MUST

Finally, when considering a style of attack against the press, the coach should resist the temptation to devise a method that requires intricate rules and maneuvers. The players have enough to think about without complicating their assignments with an assortment of keys and rules. If assignments are kept simple and the team uses sound, basic basketball fundamentals, the press need not be the monster it's cracked up to be.

GAINING THE INBOUND PRESS AGAINST ZONE PRESSURE

Many teams contest the inbound pass before they begin double teaming and trapping tactics. The following represent some methods of gaining the inbound pass from the different alignments described later *(Diagrams 10-3, 4, 5, 6)*:

One Man

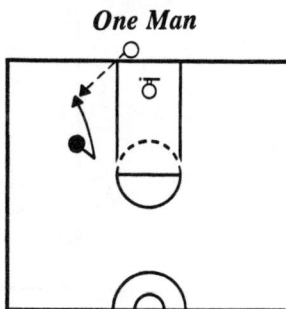

If a team is seriously contesting the inbound pass, one man may not be adequate. The most important thing is that he not give ground to pressure. He must go *at* the man pressuring him, make contact and push away (legally of course). The inbounder must remember that he has the entire baseline on which to roam, giving him some flexibility and decreasing the defense's area of influence.

Diagram 10-3

SPECIAL NOTE:

These attacks against the full court zone press are designed to work against any type of extended defense. Defensive alignments are depicted only to illustrate the offense's effectiveness and are not to be considered the only defenses against which it is effective.

Two Men

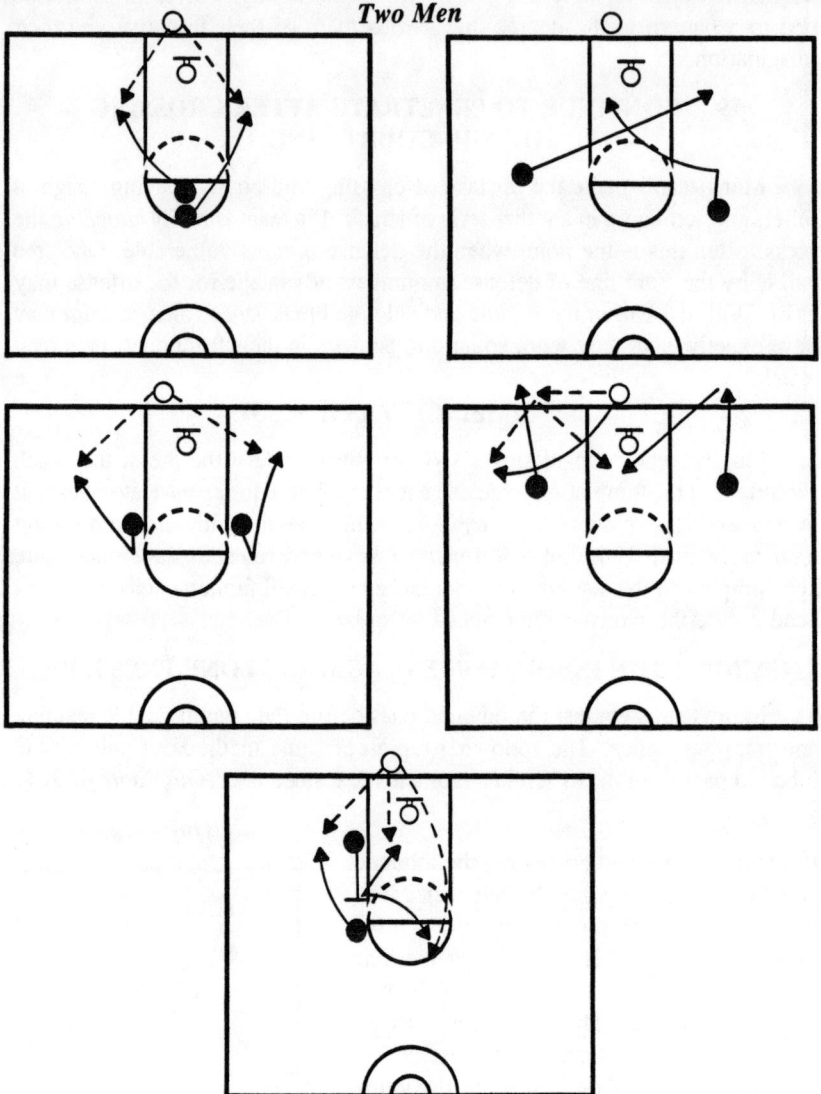

Diagram 10-4

Three Men

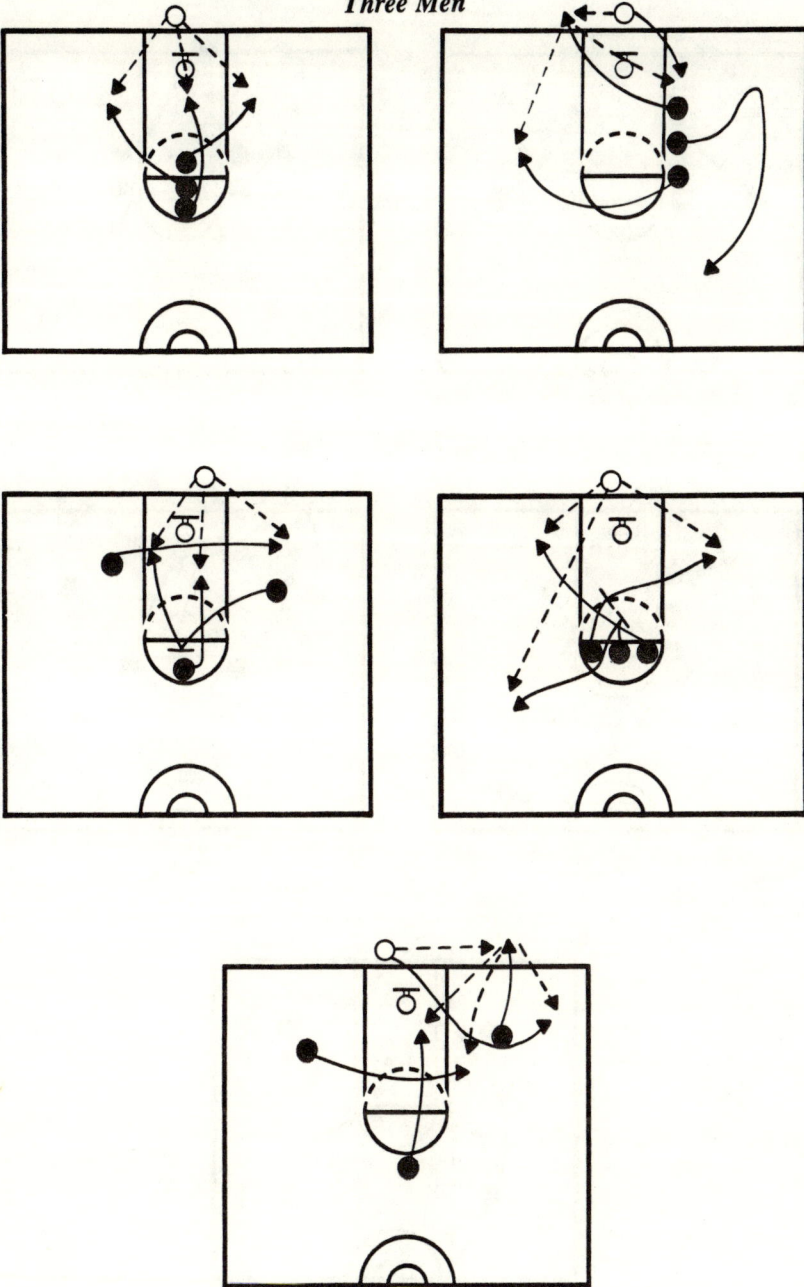

Diagram 10-5

Four Men

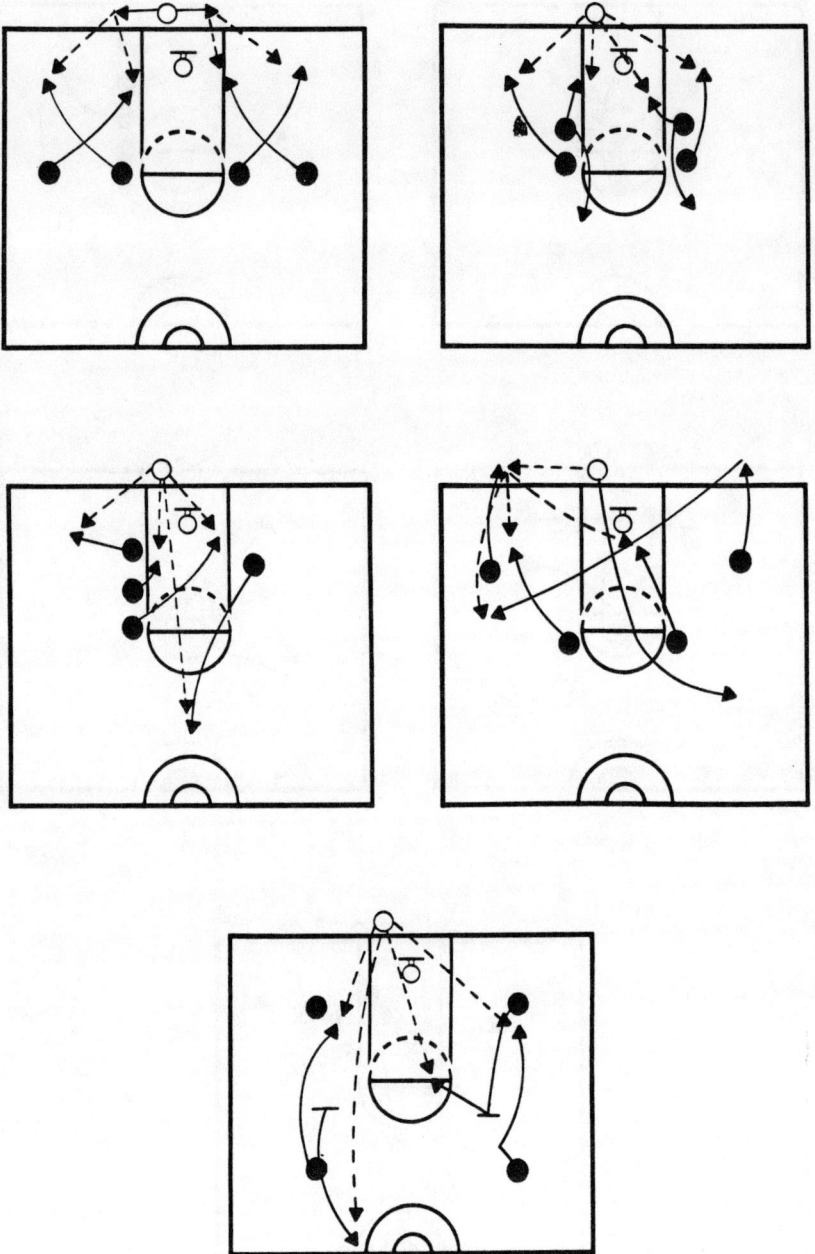

Diagram 10-6

1-2-2 ALIGNMENT AGAINST A FULL COURT ZONE PRESS

Attack number 1

2 and 3 set up in positions to clear themselves for an inbound pass. 4 and 5 go to opposite corners near mid-court in the back court. If 2 receives a pass, 3 will sprint diagonally through the middle expecting a pass anywhere along his path. 1 fills 3's vacated spot. 5 comes to the middle of the court and 4 loops across and into 5's vacated spot. This arrangement gives the man with the ball three pass possibilities. *(Diagram 10-7)*

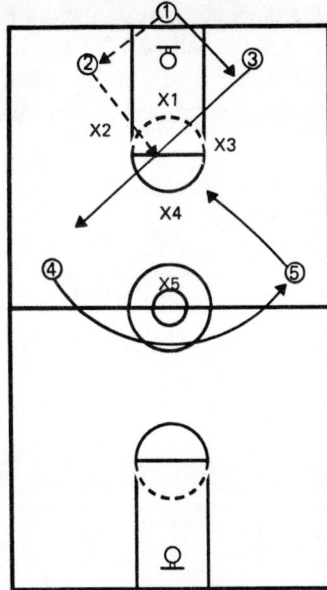

Diagram 10-7

If the ball is passed to 3, he should try to take it to the middle on a dribble. 4 goes diagonally across court to the outside break lane, and 5 rolls to the sideline away from the pass. 1 and 2 become trailers. *(Diagram 10-8)*

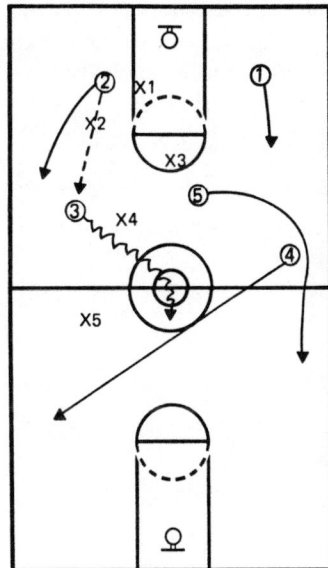

Diagram 10-8

If the ball goes to 5 in the middle, he should protect the ball, pivot and look up court. If he does not have a man on him, he can advance the ball on a dribble. If he does, he can hit either 3 or 4 at the sidelines. *(Diagram 10-9)*

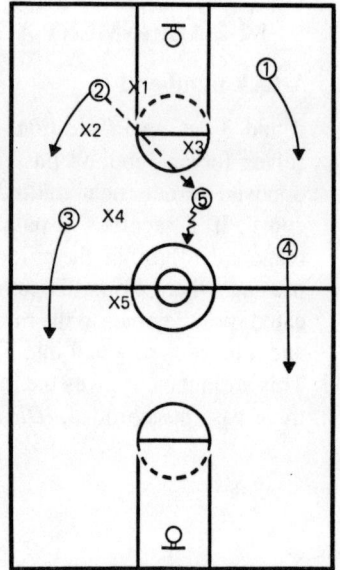

Diagram 10-9

If the passes to 3 and 5 are taken away, 1 will almost always be open. 2 can pass across to him and he can quickly fire a pass to 4 coming up to meet the ball. If possible he should take the ball to the middle on a dribble. As soon as 2 passes to 1, 5 clears out to the opposite sideline and 3 crosses to the strong sideline. *(Diagram 10-10)*

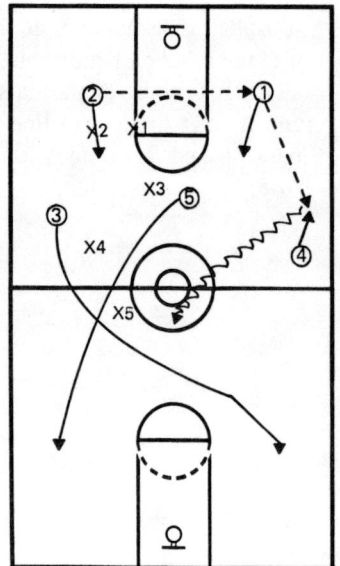

Diagram 10-10

Attack number 2

The inbound pass goes to a wing who has cleared himself (2). 1 now sprints through and goes down court. 3 crosses diagonally to a spot on the sideline on the ball side. 5 hurries up to take a pass after the area is cleared by 3. *(Diagram 10-11)*

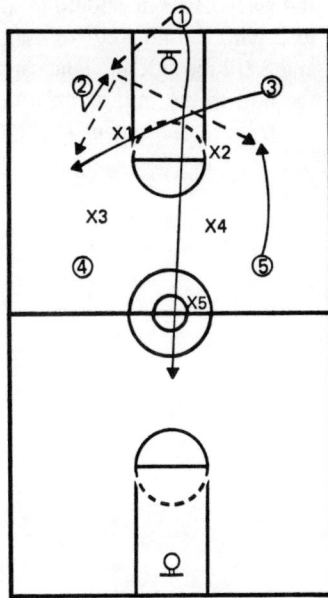

Diagram 10-11

If 2 finds that he is unable to receive an inbound pass he can cut through and move up court. 4 immediately fills his spot and receives an inbound pass. The same action as described before now takes place. 3 crosses diagonally and 5 comes up to take a pass after the area is vacated by 3. *(Diagram 10-12)*

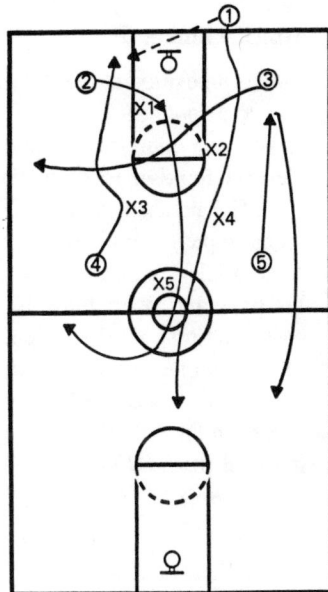

Diagram 10-12

If 4 passes to 3 he should in turn look to pass to 2 who has hooked back at the sideline. 1 and 5 fill the sideline lanes and 2 tries to take the ball to the middle on a dribble. 3 and 4 are trailers. *(Diagram 10-13)*

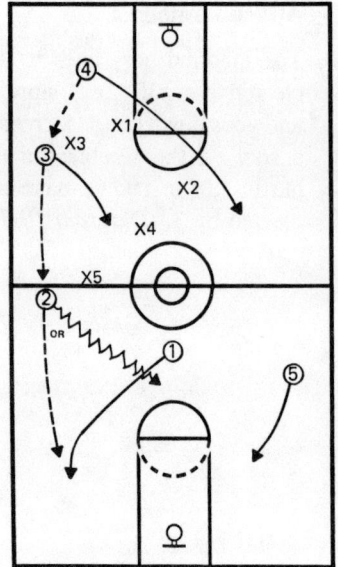

Diagram 10-13

1-1-1-2 ALIGNMENT AGAINST A FULL COURT ZONE PRESS

Attack number 1

2 takes a position at the free-throw line and 3 goes to a spot near the top of the key. 4 and 5 clear down court, with 4 staying in the middle and looking to help out after the first pass. If 2 breaks right to clear himself for the inbound pass, 3 will go left to accomplish the same goal. 1 will go away from the side of his pass and open himself up for a return pass. The man on that side (3) will clear out to the sideline. If possible, the ball should be returned to 1. 4 clears himself for a pass from 2. 5 clears downcourt favoring the side of the inbound pass. *(Diagram 10-14)*

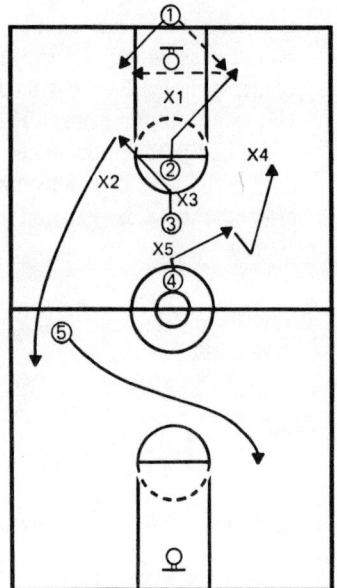

Diagram 10-14

After the pass to 1, 2 cuts diagonally to the sideline. 1 brings the ball up on a dribble until he is stopped. 1 has 2 and 4 at the sidelines to receive a pass if he is double teamed. 5 pops back to give an additional pass opportunity to 1 in the middle. *(Diagram 10-15)*

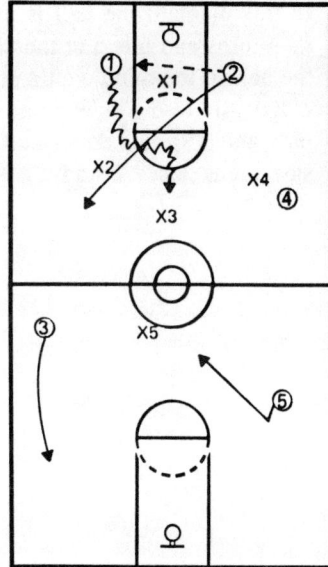

Diagram 10-15

If 2 passes the ball to 4, he should attempt to get the ball into the middle on a dribble. 3 and 5 will be at the sidelines while 2 and 1 serve as trailers. *(Diagram 10-16)*

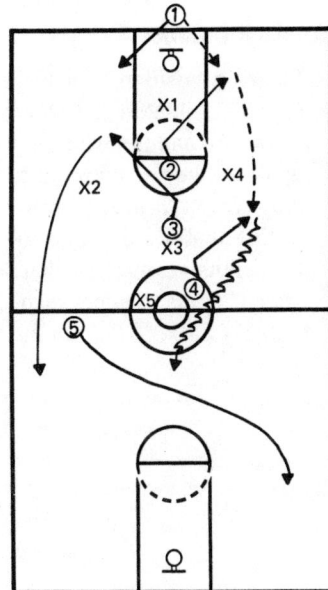

Diagram 10-16

In this diagram the ball is passed to 3. He then turns and hits 5 at the sideline. 5 takes the ball to the middle on a dribble as 4 cuts diagonally to the sideline on the side of the pass and 2 sprints downcourt to fill his outside break lane. 2 and 1 are now trailers. *(Diagram 10-17)*

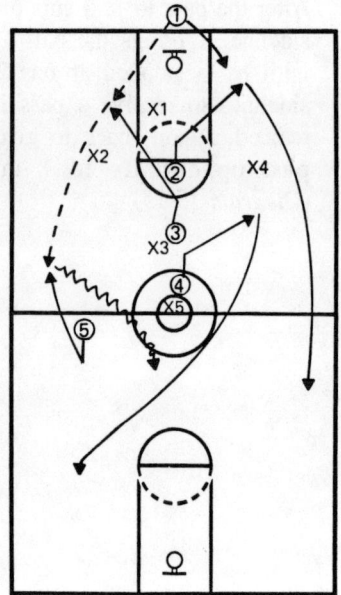

Diagram 10-17

Attack number 2

2 takes a position near the side of the lane and approximately halfway between the free throw line and the baseline. 3 starts near the top of the key. 2 pops out to the side to free himself, and 3 moves in to fill his spot expecting that 1's move to the side will draw the defensive man in that area with him. After 1's pass to either man, he moves away from his pass. *(Diagram 10-18)*

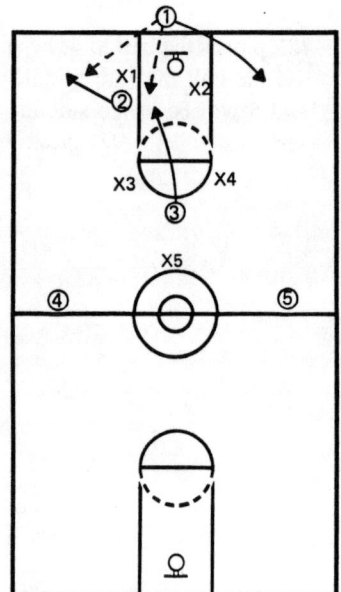

Diagram 10-18

If 3 receives the ball in the middle, he has the three pass possibilities: 4 to his right, 5 straight ahead, and 1 to his left (or in the center if a defensive adjustment dictates). The most likely pass will be to 1 as he is away from the congestion. If the ball goes to him, he should look to hit 5 at his sideline immediately. If this happens, 4 will cross diagonally looking for a deep pass as 2 fills the lane on the side away from the ball. If possible, 5 should start a dribble into the middle of the court to open up more opportunities. *(Diagram 10-19)*

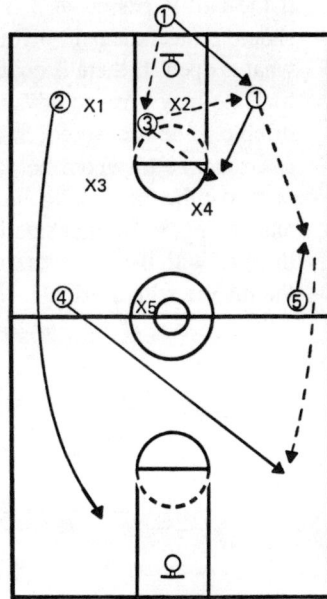

Diagram 10-19

If the ball is inbounded to 2, he will have the three passes available—to his right, in front, and to his left. 4 clears himself along the sideline for a pass. If he receives the ball, 5 should diagonally cross deep as 1 sprints to fill the sideline lane away from the ball. *(Diagram 10-20)*

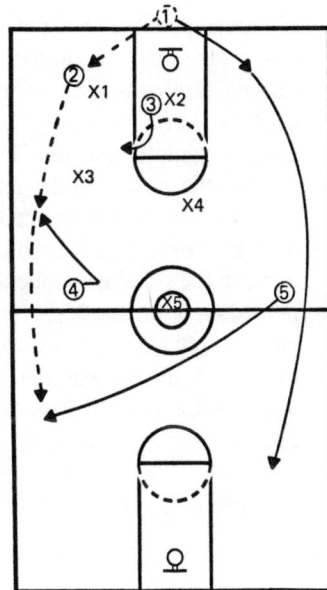

Diagram 10-20

If the ball is passed to 3 in the middle, he should protect the ball, pivot, and look to see what is open. If there is no defensive man on him, he may wish to advance the ball on a dribble. If he is covered, he has both 4 and 5 at a sideline to whom he can pass. After a pass to either man he should follow his pass and attempt to fill that sideline break lane as the man with the ball tries to get the ball into the middle with a dribble. *(Diagram 10-21)*

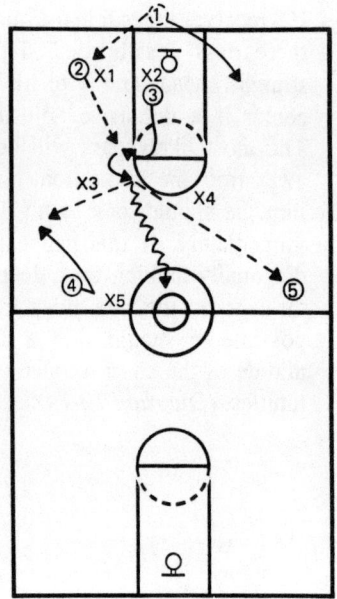

Diagram 10-21

It's quite possible that the defense will be able to shut off a pass to the sideline near the ball *and* to the man in the middle. It's very unlikely, however, that they will be able to cover 1 while doing this. 1 should be open most of the time, and the man with the ball should not become flustered knowing this. If the ball is passed to 1, he should try to move it to 5 at the sideline as quickly as possible. 4 immediately clears deep, hoping to gain a numbers advantage downcourt. 3 also hooks to an open spot in the middle to make himself available for a pass if 5 is covered. *(Diagram 10-22)*

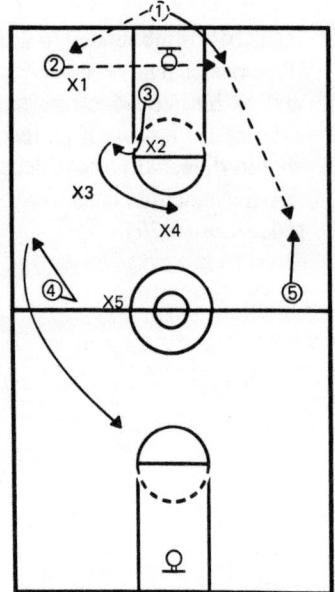

Diagram 10-22

1-3-1 ALIGNMENT AGAINST A FULL COURT ZONE PRESS

Attack number 1

2 and 4 attempt to shake themselves free for an inbound pass from 1. If possible the ball will be returned to 1. 3 steps up to be in position to set a pick for 1. *(Diagram 10-23)*

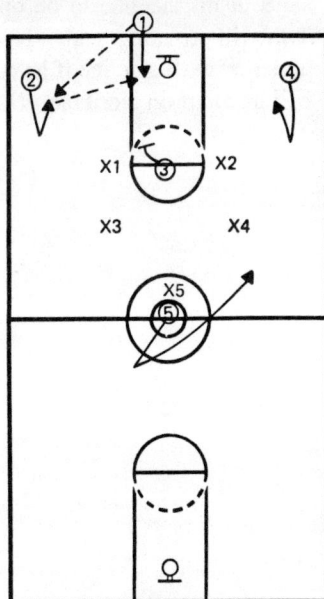

Diagram 10-23

1 immediately tries to pass to 4 if he is open. He then cuts off 3's pick, expecting a return pass after he has cleared 3's screen. After 1 goes by, 3 steps back to put himself in an open spot to receive a pass from 4 if necessary. This gives 4 three possibilities: 3, 1, and 5 coming up from the front court. 2 sprints down court in the outside break lane. *(Diagram 10-24)*

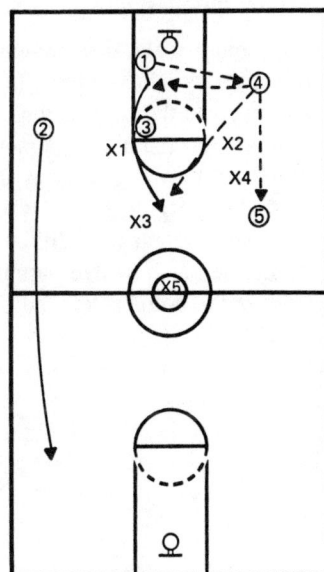

Diagram 10-24

If the pass goes to 3, 5 crosses over to take the outside lane as 1 clears down court. 4 stays at his sideline to be open for a pass. This will provide 3 with a pass possibility to a man at each sideline if he cannot bring the ball up court on a dribble. *(Diagram 10-25)*

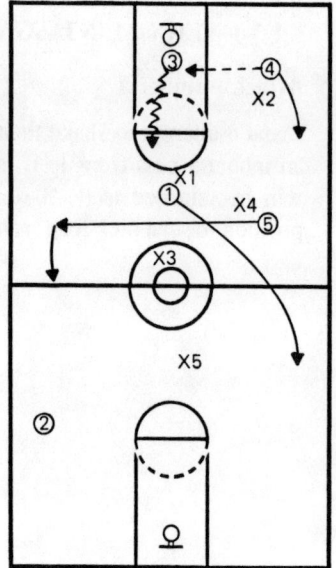

Diagram 10-25

Attack number 2

2, 3, and 4 make their moves to free themselves for an inbound pass. In this diagram 2 has received the pass, keying 3 to roll to the sideline near the ball. 4 comes to the middle of the court and 1 goes away from his pass. 5 holds his position to see where the second pass will be made. With the ball in 2's hands, he has his three pass possibilities: in front and to both his left and right. *(Diagram 10-26)*

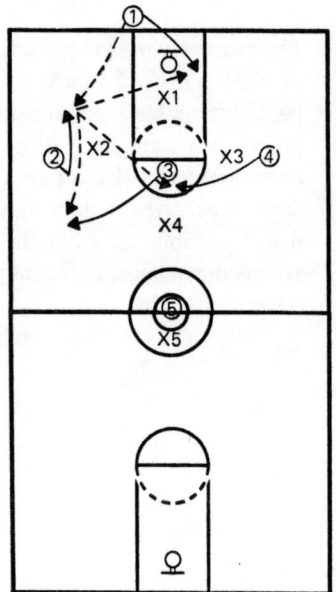

Diagram 10-26

If 2 passes to 3 at the sideline, 5 rolls deep to the sideline ahead of 3. 4 moves down court quickly to make himself available for a pass in the middle. 1 sprints down court, filling the sideline lane and 2 goes across court to fill 1's area relationship to the ball. 3 now has the same three pass possibilities as he moves down the court on a dribble. *(Diagram 10-27)*

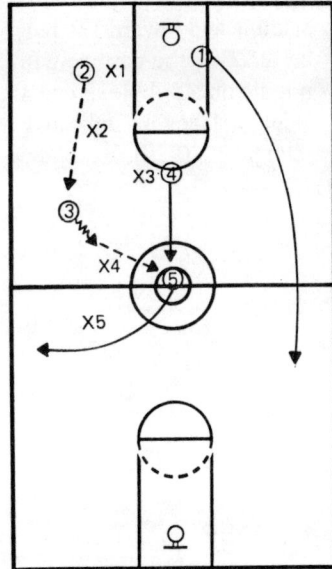

Diagram 10-27

If the ball goes to 4, he will pivot and attempt to advance the ball on a dribble. 3 and 5 are ahead of him at the sidelines. *(Diagram 10-28)*

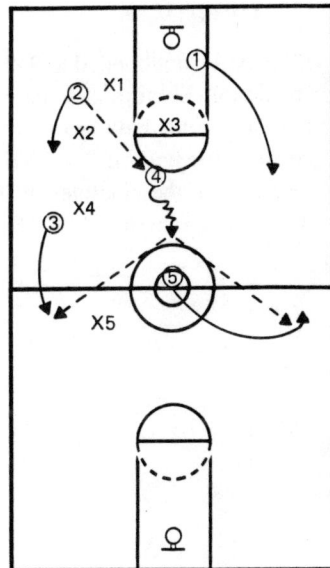

Diagram 10-28

If 2 passes across to 1, 5 will go to the sideline and toward 1 to receive a pass. After he receives the pass he will try to get to the middle on a dribble. 3 and 4 have streaked to sideline lanes as indicated in the diagram. *(Diagram 10-29)*

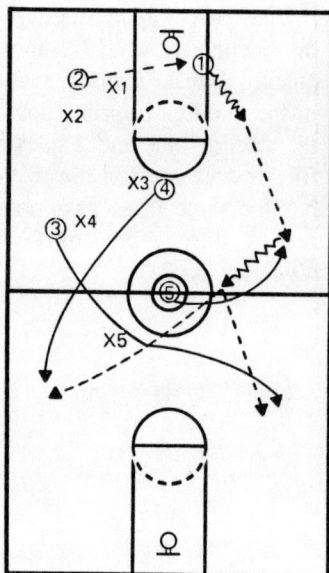

Diagram 10-29

OPTION

If the ball is inbounded to 3 in the middle, he should quickly turn and survey the situation. If he does not have a man on him, he can advance the ball on a dribble or he can pass to 2 or 4 at the sidelines or to 5 in front of him. *(Diagram 10-30)*

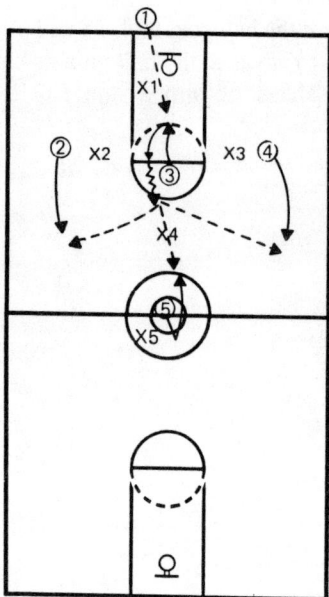

Diagram 10-30

1-1-2-1 ALIGNMENT AGAINST A FULL COURT ZONE PRESS

Attack number 1

2 takes a spot near the free-throw line and breaks either right or left to receive an inbound pass from 1. After the pass, 1 goes away from the ball to be in position to take a return pass if 2 gets double teamed. The corner man on the ball side (3) fakes down court and comes back to a spot near the sideline to receive a pass from 2. 5 shakes himself free for a pass from 3 in the middle of the court. 4 and 3 now fill the outside break lanes with 1 and 2 serving as the trailers. *(Diagram 10-31)*

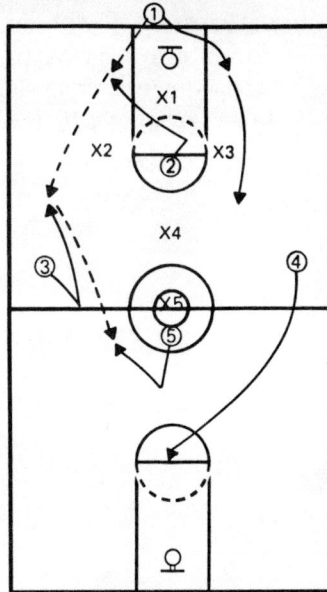

Diagram 10-31

OPTION

With the wings covered, 5 may come high to take a direct pass from 2. 3 and 4 still stay at the sidelines with 1 and 2 serving as the trailers. *(Diagram 10-32)*

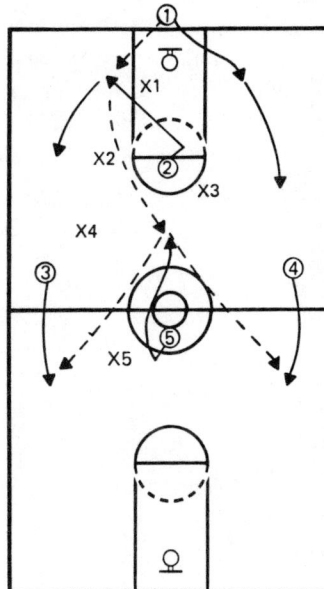

Diagram 10-32

Attack number 2

2 breaks to an open spot to receive an inbound pass from 1. As soon as 1 passes to 2
he moves away from his pass. 2 now has a
pass opportunity in front and to both his left
and right. *(Diagram 10-33)*

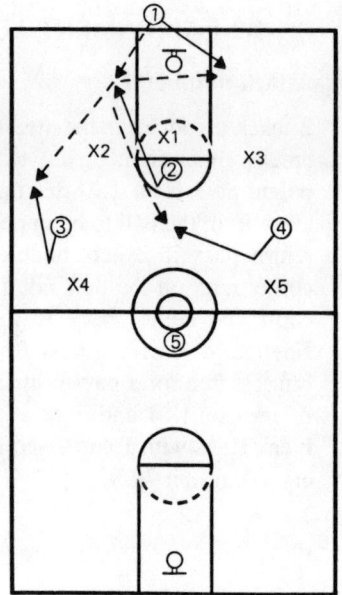

Diagram 10-33

If 2 passes to 3, 3 will now have the same
opportunities: in front and to his left and
right. 5 goes to the sideline, 4 has sprinted
down the middle, and 2 fills 4's vacated
area. 1 sprints down the sideline away from
the ball. *(Diagram 10-34)*

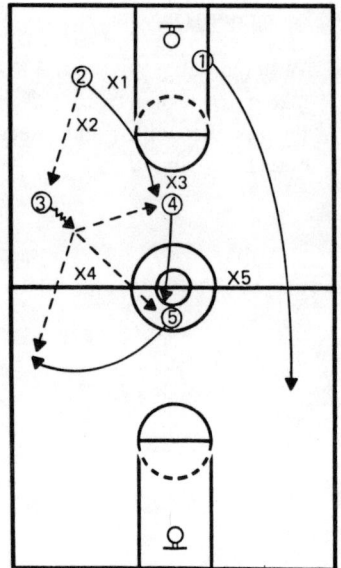

Diagram 10-34

If 2 passes to 4 in the middle, 5 rolls to the sideline and 3 stays in his sideline lane. This gives 4 two passes ahead as he attempts to advance the ball on a dribble. *(Diagram 10-35)*

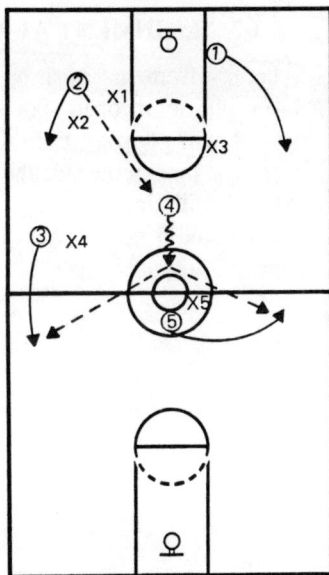

Diagram 10-35

2 can pass across to 1. 5 rolls to that sideline and comes up to meet the pass. 4 sprints down the strong sideline lane as 3 advances in his sideline lane. 5 now tries to get the ball into the middle on a dribble looking for the two men ahead of him. *(Diagram 10-36)*

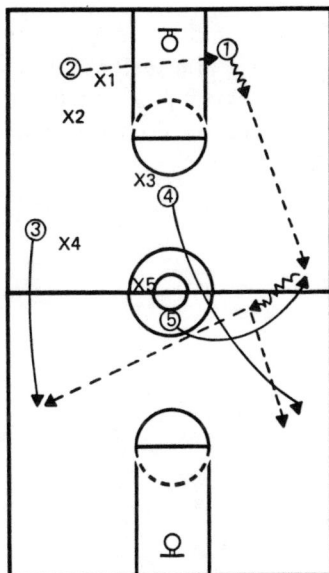

Diagram 10-36

1-1-3 ALIGNMENT AGAINST THE FULL COURT ZONE PRESS

2 breaks from his position near the free-throw line to an open spot for the inbound pass. 1 will go away from the ball after his pass. The man in the sideline lane on the ball side (3) will clear out deep. 4 comes to the sideline and 5 moves into the middle of the court. *(Diagram 10-37)*

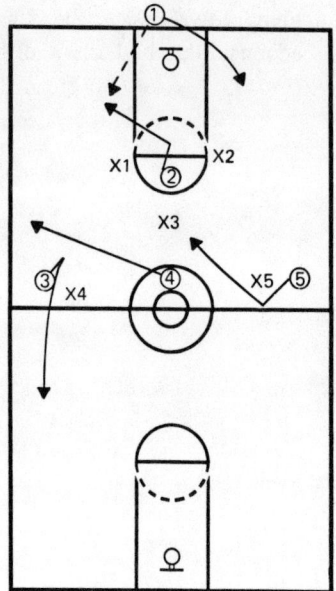

Diagram 10-37

Now 2 has a pass opportunity straight ahead (5) and to his left (1) and right (4). He also may have a pass deep to 3 if the defense has not covered deep. *(Diagram 10-38)*

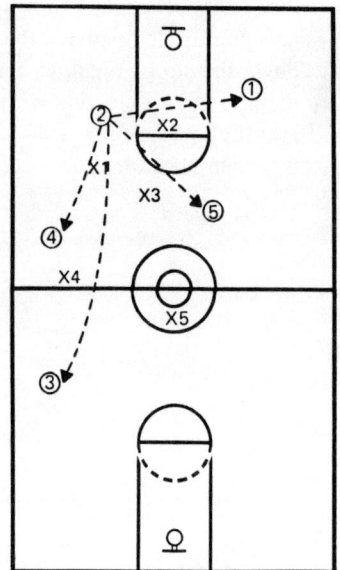

Diagram 10-38

If 2 passes to 4, 5 quickly moves down the middle to a position comparable to the one he held for 2. 4 can also hit 3 at the sideline or 1 near mid-court. *(Diagram 10-39)*

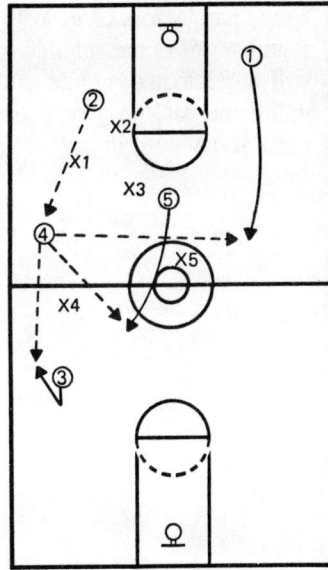

Diagram 10-39

If 2 can hit 5 in the middle, 5 should make an effort to advance the ball on a dribble or hit either 4 at the sideline or 3 who crosses the court and fills the sideline lane to 5's left. *(Diagram 10-40)*

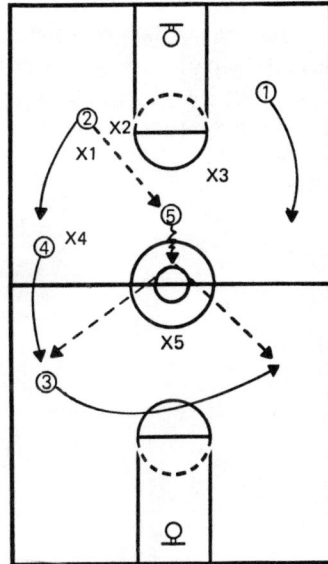

Diagram 10-40

2 may pass across court to 1. If this happens 5 will sprint to the sideline to take a pass. 2 will move to the middle of the court and 4 will come back to give 1 a pass back to his right if he gets in any trouble. *(Diagram 10-41)*

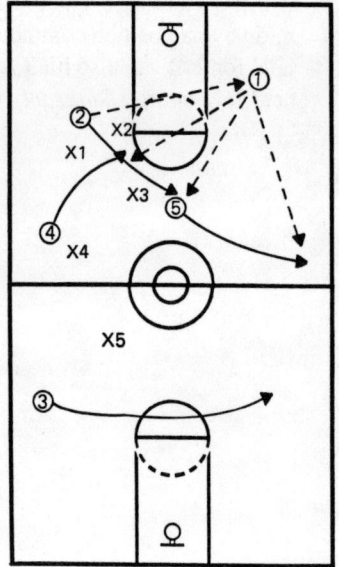

Diagram 10-41

"I" ALIGNMENT AGAINST A FULL COURT ZONE PRESS

Attack number 1

2 takes a position near the free-throw line, 3 at the top of the key, 4 near mid-court and 5 at about 3/4 court. 2 and 3 can break in either direction to receive the pass from 1. *(Diagram 10-42)*

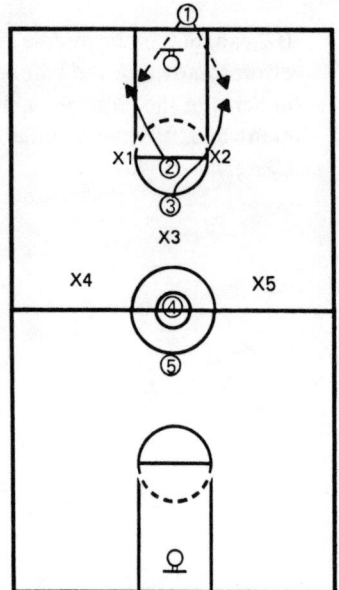

Diagram 10-42

In this example, 1 has passed to 2. 1 now cuts quickly down the middle and hooks back looking for a pass. 4 rolls to a position near the sideline on the ball side. 2 now has a pass opportunity in front and to his left and right. *(Diagram 10-43)*

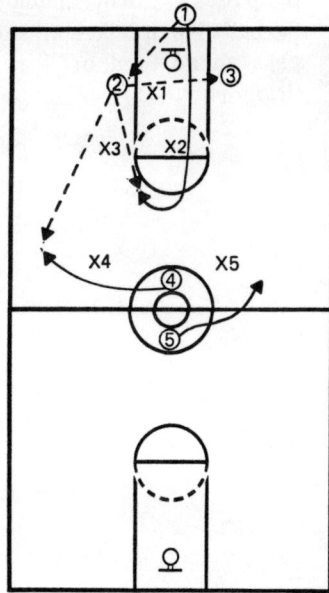

Diagram 10-43

If 2 passes to 4 at the sideline, 4 should attempt to get the ball into the middle on a dribble. As he does so, 1 will come behind him and fill the sideline lane. With the ball in the middle now, 4 can pass ahead to either 1 or 5. *(Diagram 10-44)*

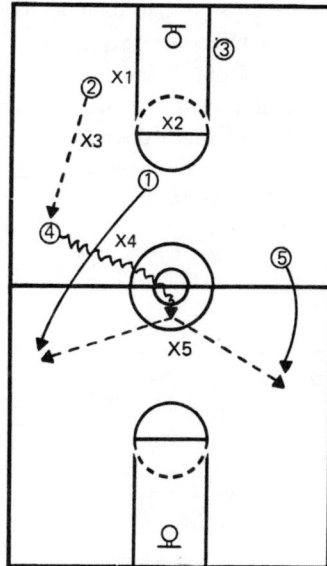

Diagram 10-44

If 2 passes to 1 in the middle, he can advance the ball on a dribble until stopped or he may pass ahead to 4 or 5 at the sidelines. *(Diagram 10-45)*

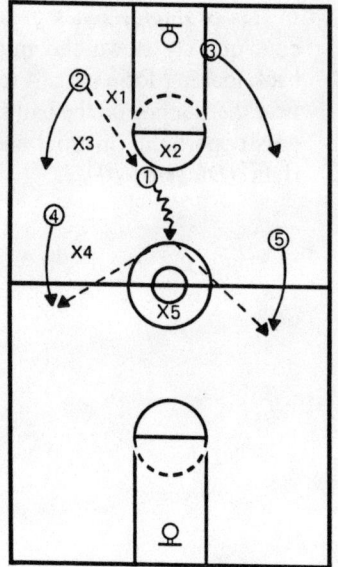

Diagram 10-45

2 may find that his most available pass is to 3. 5 will come up quickly looking for a quick pass from 3 and then try to take it to the middle on a dribble. 1 fills the sideline lane and 4 moves down court in his lane. This gives 5 two pass possibilities ahead. *(Diagram 10-46)*

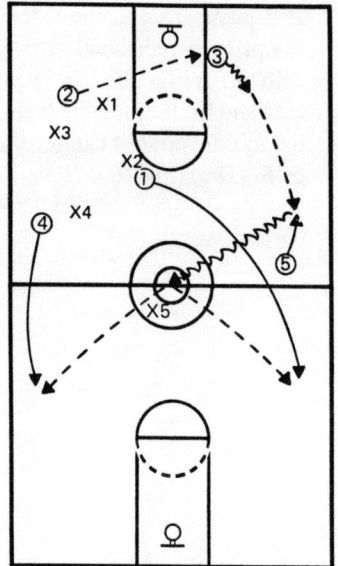

Diagram 10-46

1-4 ALIGNMENT AGAINST THE FULL COURT ZONE PRESS

The 1-4 alignment provides almost limitless variations for inbounding and maneuvering against a full court zone press. Here, 1 has inbounded to 3 breaking to an open spot. 2 moves a few steps down the sideline lane, 4 sprints deep on the ball side and 5 hooks back into the middle to free himself for a pass. 1 moves away from his pass. This gives 3 a pass in front, to his left and right, and deep. *(Diagram 10-47)*

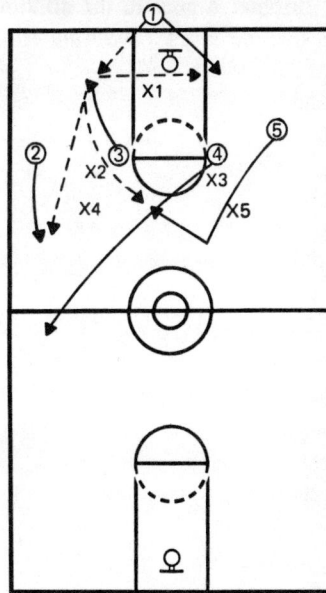

Diagram 10-47

If 3 passes to 2, 5 rolls to the sideline behind 2's dribble into the middle. 1 sprints down-court in the sideline lane and 4 moves into the middle near the free-throw line. Again, the three pass possibilities exist: ahead and to both left and right. *(Diagram 10-48)*

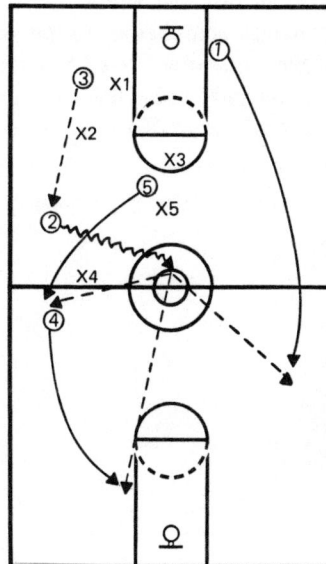

Diagram 10-48

If the ball goes to 5 in the middle, he will pivot and then try to advance the ball on a dribble. 4 goes to the middle as 1 and 2 fill sideline lanes. *(Diagram 10-49)*

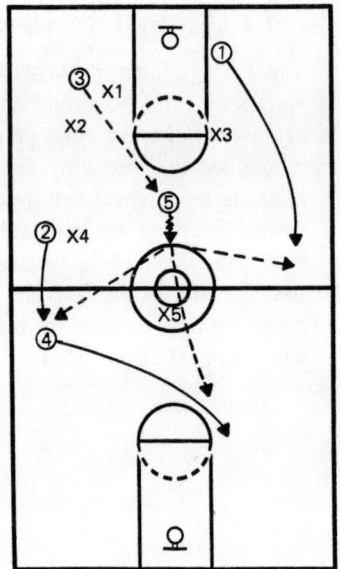

Diagram 10-49

3 can pass back across to 1. If this happens, 4 moves across court to the sideline ahead of the ball. Now 1 has 5 in the middle, 3 to his right and 4 to his left as he advances the ball. *(Diagram 10-50)*

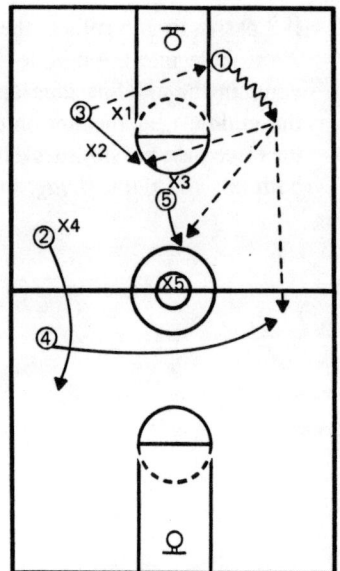

Diagram 10-50

VARIATION

Here is one of the many possible variations to the same pattern. 2 clears himself for the inbound pass. 3 now rolls to the sideline, 4 comes to the middle and 1 goes away from his pass. This produces the same pass options. *(Diagram 10-51)*

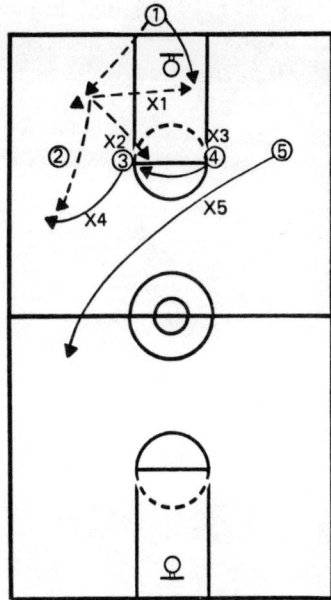

Diagram 10-51

Chapter 11

ATTACKING MID-COURT ZONE PRESSES

Attacking the mid-court zone press presents a few new problems, but basically the attack concepts used against the full court zone press are the same as would be necessary to counter mid-court pressure. First, let's deal with the differences: (1) The court is not so large and the defense is not so spread, making open areas a bit smaller and seams a bit narrower. Once the mid-court line has been crossed, a team is obviously limited to only half the area they had in which to maneuver in the full court. (2) The defense is usually more compact and conscious of the middle and the area around the lane. (3) The corners become a dangerous area where trapping can occur if teams are not careful. (4) Attack initiative may shift. In a full court press, the defense most often *reacts* to offensive movement, but in a mid-court press the defense may force the offense to react to it, particularly if the pressure does not dissolve as soon as the ball has escaped the first trap. These guiding principles should help in constructing an attack:

1. Attempt to get the ball in the middle. *All* mid-court presses are less
    effective with the ball in the middle because it opens up passing
    angles and threatens the defense on both sides of the court.

2. Spread the defense and try to draw the double team. Only then will
    a numbers advantage exist producing an open man somewhere on
    the court.

3. Use the pass! Keep dribbling to a minimum. Remember it's a *zone*
    press and it is to be attacked with quick short passes.

4. Players can't stand waiting for the pass. As is true in all offensive
    basketball, *movement* creates problems for the defense.

5. Attempt to create a situation where the ball handler has a pass ahead
    and to both his left and right if possible. When double teamed, it's
    comforting to know that there are players in areas easily seen and
    reached with a short pass.

6. Once the ball has escaped the first trap, attack! If the defense has
    been penetrated it may be a mistake to back off and set up the
    patterned attack, giving up an opportunity that's hard to come by.

7. Crash the boards! Having extended and spread itself, the defense is
    not in a strong rebounding position, nor is it able to block out
    effectively.

8. Slide smoothly into a patterned offense. It is advisable that you
    devise a method of getting into a standard attack quickly and effi-
    ciently if a shot does not occur. To have to set up takes time, and it
    allows the defense to recover and position itself. An overload situa-
    tion is easy to produce and from there a patterned attack can de-
    velop.

SPECIAL NOTE:

These methods of combating mid-court pressure defenses are only illus-
trations of the principles presented in the introductions. You will want to
devise your own method of attack from an alignment that best suits your style
of play.

1 draws the double team. In all probability 3 will be covered in the middle, but after a pass to 2, 3 may be open. If the ball goes to him he turns and faces the basket. 4 and 5 dive to the low posts and 3 attempts to penetrate as he looks for the open man. *(Diagram 11-1)*

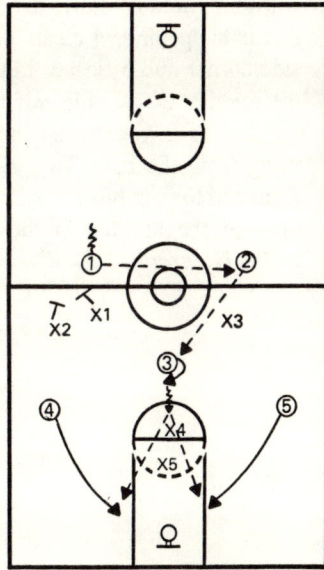

Diagram 11-1

If 3 is still covered in the middle, he should move to the strong sideline drawing his coverage with him. 4 immediately fills his vacated spot. The pass may go to either man. If it goes to 3, 5 will hook into the corner, and 4 will roll to the low post looking for a pass at the basket. If the ball is passed to 4 in the middle, 5 will cross the lane to the low post on the other side and 3 will sprint down to the baseline. *(Diagram 11-2)*

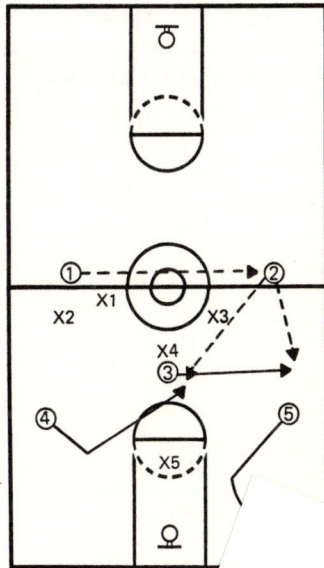

Diagram 11

1 dribbles until he draws the double team. As
this is happening, 4 clears out to the strong
side corner and 5 flashes to the open spot in
the middle. 3 frees himself for a pass at the
sideline as 2 goes to an outside open area
away from the ball. This gives 1 a pass in
front and to both his left and right. 4 could be
open at the baseline if the defense covers
high. *(Diagram 11-3)*

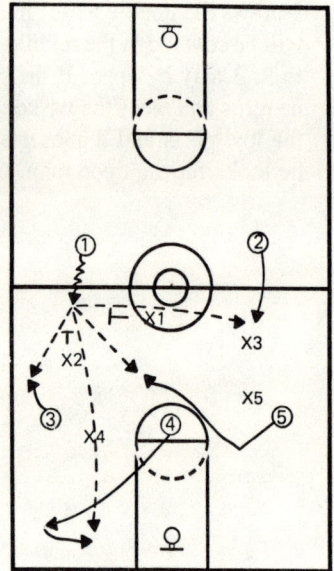

Diagram 11-3

If 1 passes to 3 at the sideline, 4 moves to the
strong side corner, 5 goes to an open spot at
the high post, and 2 makes himself available
for a pass in the middle. *(Diagram 11-4)*

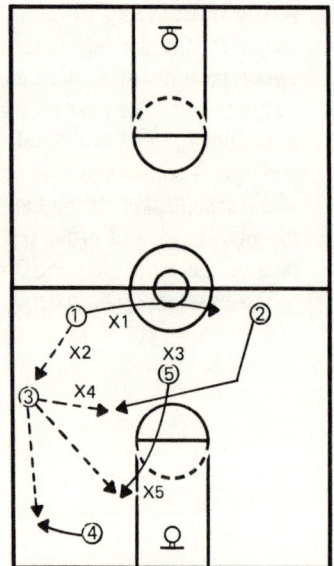

Diagram 11-4

If the ball goes to 5 in the middle, 4 will cross the lane to the low post on the weak side. 3 now dives to the strongside low post. 5 now has two passes near the basket as he attempts to penetrate. *(Diagram 11-5)*

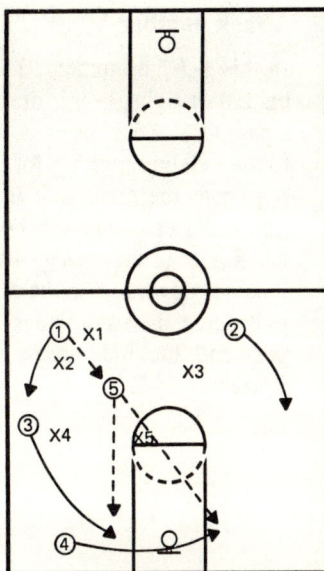

Diagram 11-5

If the defense covers the ball side, 1 may have to pass across to 2. 2 quickly dribbles away and down as 4 crosses over to the corner on the ball side. 5 flashes to the low post and 3 comes to the high post. Now 2 has four pass possibilities from this overloaded situation. *(Diagram 11-6)*

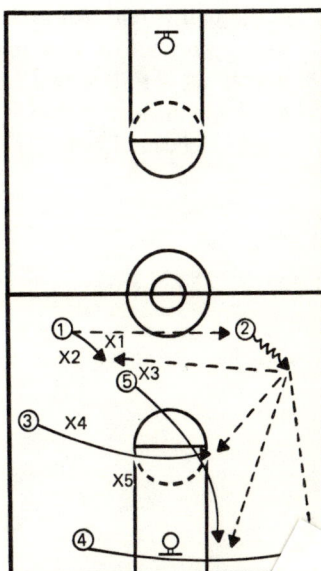

Diagram 11-6

Attack number 1

In this 1-2-2 alignment, 1 can pass to either his left or right. In this diagram he has made a pass to 2. After his pass, 1 will cut through to the sideline looking for a return pass as 4 pops into the open spot in the middle. If 2 hits 4, 3 drops down to a point even with him and 5 goes to the corner. 4 will try to hit 3. If 3 passes down to 5 in the corner, an overload will occur as 4 continues down to the low post and 1 comes across to the high post. *(Diagram 11-7)*

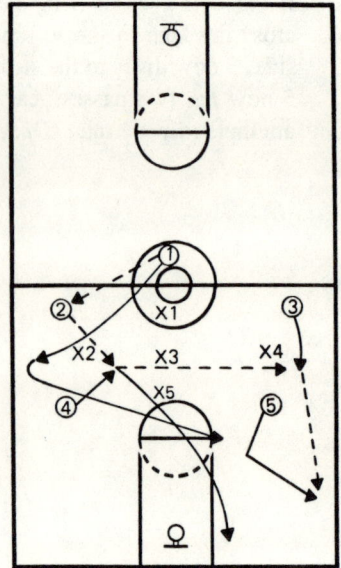

Diagram 11-7

If the ball is returned to 1 at the sideline, 5 will come across and into the strongside corner as 4 rolls down to the low post. 3 moves to the high post. Once again, an overload has been effected. *(Diagram 11-8)*

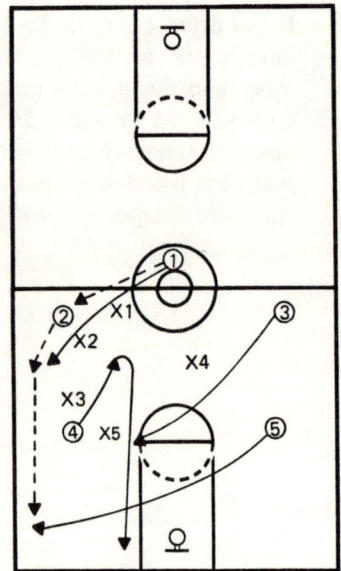

Diagram 11-8

Attack number 2

In this 1-2-2 attack the point man (1) can pass to either side. In this diagram he has passed to 2. This keys 2 to cut diagonally across court to the sideline in front of the ball, 5 to come to an open spot in the middle and 4 to step down to the baseline on the ball side. 1 moves away from his pass. This now provides 2 with a pass to a man in front of him and to both his left and right. *(Diagram 11-9)*

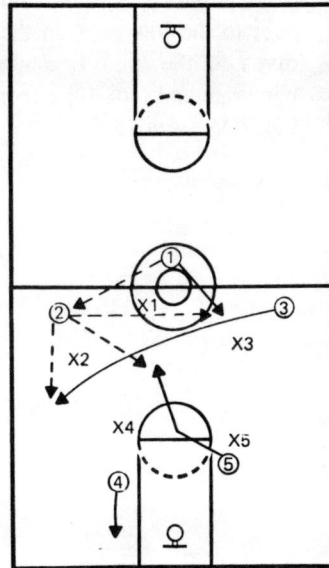

Diagram 11-9

If 2 passes to 3, 3 will immediately try to get the ball to 4 stepping out to the corner. 5 rolls to the basket looking for a pass, and 2 drops down to the high post. An overload is not effected, and a patterned attack can begin if no shot is available. *(Diagram 11-10)*

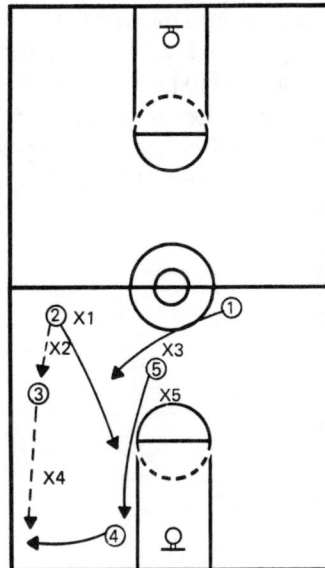

Diagram 11-10

If 2 can pass to 5 in the middle, 4 will cross over to the low post on the other side as 3 dives to the basket. 5 should attempt to penetrate and look for either man at the basket. *(Diagram 11-11)*

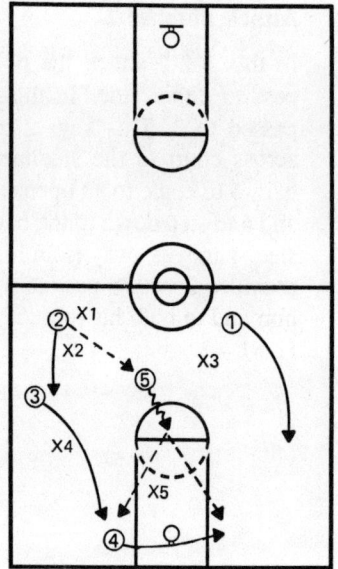

Diagram 11-11

If the men on the ball side are covered, 2 can pass back to 1. 1 dribbles to the sideline looking to hit 4 moving into the corner on his side. After the pass to 4, 5 rolls to the basket and 3 flashes to the high post. Again an overload is in evidence. *(Diagram 11-12)*

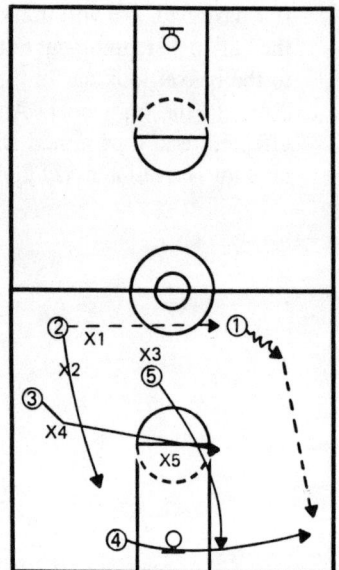

Diagram 11-12

VARIATION

To vary the pattern 1 can move into the middle after his pass and 3 can pop back to 1's spot. Now 4 will step to the sideline as 5 drops to the baseline. The spots are now filled and a pass to the open man can be made. *(Diagram 11-13)*

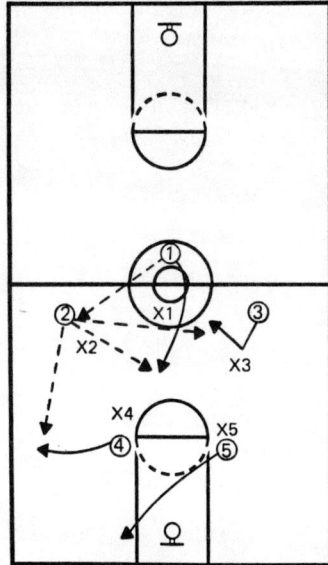

Diagram 11-13

INDEX

221